Editor-in-Chief and Founder:
    Lyndon H. LaRouche, Jr.
Editorial Board: *Lyndon H. LaRouche, Jr. , Helga
    Zepp-LaRouche, Robert Ingraham, Tony
    Papert, Gerald Rose, Dennis Small, Jeffrey
    Steinberg, William Wertz*
Co-Editors: *Robert Ingraham, Tony Papert*
Technology: *Marsha Freeman*
Transcriptions: *Katherine Notley*
Ebooks: *Richard Burden*
Graphics: *Alan Yue*
Photos: *Stuart Lewis*
Circulation Manager: *Stanley Ezrol*

INTELLIGENCE DIRECTORS
Economics: *Marcia Merry Baker, Paul Gallagher*
History: *Anton Chaitkin*
Ibero-America: *Dennis Small*
Russia and Eastern Europe: *Rachel Douglas*
United States: *Debra Freeman*

INTERNATIONAL BUREAUS
Bogotá: *Miriam Redondo*
Berlin: *Rainer Apel*
Copenhagen: *Tom Gillesberg*
Lima: *Sara Madueño*
Melbourne: *Robert Barwick*
Mexico City: *Gerardo Castilleja Chávez*
New Delhi: *Ramtanu Maitra*
Paris: *Christine Bierre*
Stockholm: *Ulf Sandmark*
United Nations, N.Y.C.: *Leni Rubinstein*
Washington, D.C.: *William Jones*
Wiesbaden: *Göran Haglund*

ON THE WEB
e-mail: eirns@larouchepub.com
www.larouchepub.com
www.executiveintelligencereview.com
www.larouchepub.com/eiw
Webmaster: *John Sigerson*
Assistant Webmaster: *George Hollis*
Editor, Arabic-language edition: *Hussein Askary*

EIR (ISSN 0273-6314) *is published weekly
(50 issues), by EIR News Service, Inc.,
P.O. Box 17390, Washington, D.C. 20041-0390.
(703) 297-8434*

European Headquarters: E.I.R. GmbH, Postfach
Bahnstrasse 9a, D-65205, Wiesbaden, Germany
Tel: 49-611-73650
Homepage: http://www.eir.de
e-mail: info@eir.de
Director: Georg Neudecker

Montreal, Canada: 514-461-1557
eir@eircanada.ca

Denmark: EIR - Danmark, Sankt Knuds Vej 11,
basement left, DK-1903 Frederiksberg, Denmark.
Tel.: +45 35 43 60 40, Fax: +45 35 43 87 57. e-mail:
eirdk@hotmail.com.

Mexico City: EIR, Sor Juana Inés de la Cruz 242-2
Col. Agricultura C.P. 11360
Delegación M. Hidalgo, México D.F.
Tel. (5525) 5318-2301
eirmexico@gmail.com

Copyright: ©2018 EIR News Service. All rights
reserved. Reproduction in whole or in part without
permission strictly prohibited.

Canada Post Publication Sales Agreement
#40683579

Postmaster: Send all address changes to *EIR*, P.O.
Box 17390, Washington, D.C. 20041-0390.

Signed articles in *EIR* represent the views of the authors,
and not necessarily those of the Editorial Board.

Schiller Institute Conference Intervenes To Shape History

Upcoming Trump-Putin Summit Can Shift the World Toward New Paradigm

This is the edited transcript of the June 27, 2018 Schiller Institute New Paradigm webcast, an interview with the founder of the Schiller Institutes, Helga Zepp-LaRouche. She was interviewed by Harley Schlanger. A video *of the webcast is available.*

Harley Schlanger: Hello, I'm Harley Schlanger from the Schiller Institute. Welcome to our weekly international webcast with our founder and President Helga Zepp-LaRouche.

Trump-Putin Summit Is On

Well, it appears that the long-awaited summit between President Donald Trump and President Vladimir Putin is about to take place. The arrangements were announced today—not the specific details that everyone's so focussed on, but the fact that they will be meeting. Nearly two years after the FBI launched the "Get Trump Task Force" under James Comey, with Peter Strzok and others, Presidents Trump and Putin reached an agreement to have that summit meeting.

This is obviously an extremely significant event, Helga, and we'd like your thoughts.

Helga Zepp-LaRouche: I think it's very important. There are still speculations where the meeting will take place. It's said that Austria is offering Vienna; the Finns are offering Helsinki, but it may also take place at the FIFA World Cup in Moscow. Whatever the venue, I think it's of strategic importance. Trump now feels somewhat freed, with Russiagate turning into Mueller-gate, and with the very successful Singapore summit. I think this is a very, very important development.

Clinically speaking, I want to mention that the German conservative daily, *Die Welt,* says this summit

Vladimir Putin receiving John Bolton at the Kremlin, June 27, 2018.

could create a catastrophe: The danger exists that Trump and Putin might make an agreement, whereby NATO maneuvers in Eastern Europe are reduced and then Trump would portray himself as the big peace-maker. [laughs] That shows you how absolutely crazy these neo-liberal/neo-conservatives are, on both sides of the Atlantic. What could anyone who wants to see peace, not war, better wish for than that Russia and the United States—which after all are the two most powerful nuclear forces on the planet—come to a strategic agreement?

So, this is a very important, good development. This summit will now occur after the NATO summit and after Trump's short trip to Great Britain. My hunch is that the two presidents will hit it off very well, because they both have a better understanding of the strategic situation, than their critics. So that is good news.

Schlanger: The other important point is that as they were moving toward this meeting, the Russiagate scandal continued to be the focus of the media, in spite of

James Mattis and Wei Fenghe review Chinese troops, Beijing, June 27, 2018.

there being nothing to it. The whole point of Russiagate was to prevent Trump from meeting with Putin. You had said some time ago, that if President Trump were to follow through with his intention and meet with Putin, this would constitute a major defeat for the enforcers of global geopolitics. They are certainly reacting with squawks and screaming. But, Helga, I'm sure that's not going to stop the two Presidents from getting together.

Zepp-LaRouche: No. I think there is absolutely no reason to think that the progress will be stopped. National Security Advisor John Bolton is currently in Moscow. I think he may have met with Putin himself, but for sure with Foreign Minister Lavrov. This summit is on a very good track.

Mattis in China

Schlanger: Bolton's Moscow meetings are occurring simultaneously with the continuing offensive of, what you might call, the Eurasian perspective: Today, Secretary of Defense General James Mattis was in China. I think he met with President Xi. Is that right?

Zepp-LaRouche: Yes, he met with Xi Jinping. They said that the purpose of their meeting was strategic trust-building and the expansion of military-to-military contact. Mattis also met with China's Minister of Defense, Wei Fenghe, and invited him to the Pentagon. This is exactly what should happen, having increasing

cooperation among the largest powers in the world: the United States, China, and Russia—and as we discussed earlier, there is also some slightly slower motion from India, to come to such an agreement. India has a good relationship with the United States, and with Russia—now they are working more closely with China.

I can only repeat: Those people who are used to thinking in terms of geopolitical blueprints, or paradigms, should understand that in this world with so many problems and so many urgent tasks to solve, the best thing is for the large powers to do is to find a strategic understanding between them, and then, hopefully, work together to begin to solve the problems of the past. Those among us who are still caught up in the old, geopolitical, zero-sum game—one wins, the other one must lose—harbor a completely ridiculous, old-fashioned, outdated idea. At the beginning of the year, I called for this year to become the year when geopolitics is overcome. With China's New Silk Road, you already have a win-win model of relations, in which everybody wins. So I urge people to rethink the way they look at the world.

Pompeo to North Korea

Schlanger: There seems to be some very significant motion with North Korea. Secretary of State Mike Pompeo will be going there; I think there's a summit coming up in July. So it does appear that in the aftermath of Singapore, things are moving in the right direction.

Zepp-LaRouche: Absolutely. This meeting in mid-July is very exciting. The two Koreas will discuss the western rail line from South Korea, through North Korea, all the way to the Chinese connection. Shortly after that meeting, there will be another meeting to discuss the eastern track that will connect the South Korean port city of Busan all the way north to the Trans-Siberian Railroad.

As we have always said, if the North Korean and South Korean engineers are building railroads together, then we will have a concrete way to overcome the war danger. So I think this is playing out very well. It certainly is thanks to Trump, and to China and Russia—this is one good example of how the world can be improved, if people work together for the common good.

A European 'Defense Force'?

Schlanger: On the other hand, the geopoliticians are still at it: The European Union has just adopted a proposal for a European defense force. Do they think this will replace NATO, because the U.S. is going to leave? Or, what? What can they possibly be thinking? Americans don't understand it.

Zepp-LaRouche: It's not the entire EU. Since every EU member nation couldn't be won over to the scheme, nine EU nations decided to create a European defense mechanism, outside of the EU. Germany and France are pushing this; Macron was the main instigator, but it is now backed by Merkel. If they start doing that, with so much disunity on so many issues—if they start building mechanisms outside of the EU—in my view, they are taking one big step toward the final dissolution of the EU. They are undermining the authority of the EU that is already near zero. So, I think this is a very dubious development.

This defense mechanism is supposed to come into being in 2021, but a lot can happen in the meantime. Maybe some completely different conceptions can be put on the table such as the earlier idea of the integration of Eurasia from Vladivostok to Lisbon. That would be a much better conception, which should also eventually be broadened to include the United States.

This maneuver shows the evil intention of the authors of this idea, but I don't think it's necessarily going to happen.

Whither the Upcoming EU Summit?

Schlanger: And there will be an EU summit coming up later this week. What are they going to be talking about there? Obviously, there's the refugee crisis, which as I understand it, is completely unresolved. What's your sense of what's going to come out of this summit?

Zepp-LaRouche: It could lead to a real clash, in which case, the fate of Merkel, the Chancellor of Germany, could take a sudden turn—in other words, she could lose power, or quickly thereafter in any case. The

EU

Jean-Claude Juncker (right) and Donald Tusk (center) at a European Council meeting in Brussels, June 29, 2018.

proposals on the table are disgusting. The only idea coming from there is a plan to militarize the refugee crisis by increasing the Frontex (EU border guard) deployment, up to 10,000. European Parliament President Antonio Tajani has proposed spending EU6 billion to lock down the Mediterranean route. Various people, including Austria's Chancellor Kurz, Italy's Interior Minister Salvini, and others are calling for so-called "disembarkment centers," identification centers to be set up outside of the territory of the European Union. Others are calling for camps inside the European Union.

The Prime Minister of Albania told the German tabloid *Bild*, "We will never accept those camps for European refugees." It would mean, he said, "unloading desperate people who no one wants, anywhere like toxic waste." So they will absolutely not do that. Even Libya has said they don't want any camps in Libya, but they want such camps south of the Libyan border, in Chad, in Niger, other countries—an obvious nightmare.

I think many people saw the horrifying pictures—I don't know if they're true, because the Algerian government claims they are not true—but supposedly there are many eyewitnesses and videos of people who say that over the past fourteen months, the Algerian government dumped more than 13,000 refugees into the Sahara, without food or water, without cell phones, without money, and many of them died.

Now, I cannot say if this is fake news or true, but even if it's not true, it reflects the truth of the dire situation. Many, many people have died in the Sahara of thirst; many have drowned in the Mediterranean,—

Interdicting refugees in Joint Operation Triton, 2017.

the extension of the New Silk Road into Africa—that all such bad approaches will fail.

We are looking at a tremendous moral crisis of the European establishment, and we are campaigning very actively to turn this around. The solution does exist.

Schlanger: Your proposal, for the adoption of the Singapore model, which you just described—the collaboration of Europe with China in developing the nations of Africa—has been given fairly wide circulation. It's getting out in Europe and the United States, in Latin America; and, as you keep reporting, a number of countries are moving toward full collaboration with the New Silk Road. Do you see this as a possibility to come up at the EU summit, or is this still being blocked by the people who are clinging to the old geopolitics?

Zepp-LaRouche: I think that this EU, in its present composition—the people in charge are so wedded to the neo-liberal model, to the idea that the world has to be organized in such a way that the markets determine everything, and that speculators become richer and the majority of people should take the burden of austerity—I don't see any among these bureaucrats who would be capable of changing and recognizing that this Western model is about to collapse. But that doesn't mean that the idea cannot be put on the agenda.

really an unknown figure because probably many of the boats have simply disappeared. This is absolutely terrible.

The East European countries didn't even go to the June 24 mini-summit called for by Merkel last Sunday. I don't think the so-called European solution is possible, which is what Merkel is insisting on. Horst Seehofer, the head of the CSU and the Interior Minister, has given her until July 1—that's Sunday—to come up with a European solution. If that does not happen, he has said that he will unilaterally start to close the border between Austria and Germany. in which case, Merkel has the choice: either to capitulate, in which case the SPD may lead the coalition government; or, to kick out Seehofer as Interior Minister, in which case, the CSU would leave the coalition. Either way, there certainly will be a government crisis.

This demonstrates that any approach to solving the refugee crisis that tolerates power-seeking, or power-grabbing motives—in which political figures attempt to keep their positions and their power, and rather than addressing the problem of the refugees with the intent to develop Africa, to develop the Middle East, and to do that in concert with the offer of China to cooperate in

You could have a situation where any number of European countries could call such an emergency summit in July, or in August. One could take such a proposal to the UN General Assembly in New York to put this on the agenda. In the meantime, a "coalition of the willing" could be brought together—to give that horrible phrase a more positive meaning—and such a group could start moving in a positive direction.

Given that the Spirit of the New Silk Road is gaining so much support among industry, and among small and medium-size enterprises, and that so many people have already recognized that there is this fantastic new dynamic in the world, I'm optimistic that eventually we can turn things around.

I'm now having the pleasure of reading a very nice book published by the Schiller Institute. It's called *The*

New Silk Road Becomes the World Land-Bridge, Vol. II, just fresh off the press. It contains all the conceptions necessary to immediately start these large-scale development projects. I think there may be more people who would want to know what is in this book.

Schlanger: People can find out about it on the Schiller Institute website. I think it is important for people to be reading that report, to discuss the material and to pass it around.

Alexandria Ocasio-Cortez

U.S. Midterm Primary Elections

We have one final story, Helga, in which I'm sure you have some interest: the primaries for the November 2018 midterm elections in the United States. A couple months ago, the Democrats were forecasting a "blue wave," that is, that the Democrats would have a big comeback, that Trump was finished. Two results stand out from yesterday's voting. In the race for governor of South Carolina, at the last minute Trump endorsed the current Governor, McMaster. The media said Trump was making a mistake; that McMaster was going to lose. In fact, the voters turned out in support of the person Trump was supporting, McMaster, who did win. In New York State, the number-four Democrat in the U.S. House, 10-term Representative Joseph Crowley, who had been mooted as a possible replacement for Nancy Pelosi, was defeated by first-time candidate, the 28-year-old Alexandria Ocasio-Cortez, a virtual unknown, who had been a Bernie Sanders campaign worker! I guess this shows the insurgency against the establishment continues in both parties in the United States.

Joseph Crowley

Zepp-LaRouche: The tweets Trump put out were quite good. About Crowley's defeat, he said, "Wow! Big Trump Hater Congressman Joe Crowley, who many expected was going to take Nancy Pelosi's place, just LOST his primary election. In other words, he's out! That is a big one that nobody saw happening. Perhaps he should have been nicer, and more respectful, to his President!" Whereas Crowley's campaign spent $3 million, this 28-year-old woman who won the primary, beat him with only $300,000, campaigning on the fact that Crowley was a tool of Wall Street. This was the main reason she won the primary.

With these primary election results, it becomes more visible that not everything is controlled by the financial oligarchy. Money can no longer buy every seat, which had been the norm for a long time. There is an opportunity to really change the situation in the world for the better.

Join the Schiller Institute!

I want to conclude by again asking everyone listening to join the Schiller Institute. Join a Renaissance movement, and help us circulate these ideas, so that more people can share and join in the optimism that man *is* indeed greater than his destiny. If many people of good join forces together—as Schiller says in his writings about the revolt of the Netherlands against Spanish domination—you can bring down the arm of the strongest tyrant by uniting for the good.

So please, unite with us, and let's really move civilization into a better domain.

Schlanger: Helga, thank you for continuing to be a beacon of optimism even as we're surrounded by naysayers and pessimists, some of whom are beginning to get this message, and who should do their best to not just watch our webcasts, but become active with the Schiller Institute. So, till next week, Helga, we'll see you then.

Zepp-LaRouche: Bye-bye.

EIRContents

www.larouchepub.com   Volume 45, Number 27, July 6, 2018

EIRNS/Christopher Lewis

Cover This Week

June 30-July 1 Schiller Institute Conference in Bad Soden, Germany.

HISTORIC SCHILLER INSTITUTE CONFERENCE

Opens Door for U.S.A. and Europe To Join the New Paradigm

by Harley Schlanger

July 3—The timing could not have been more propitious for the June 30-July 1 Schiller Institute conference on, since it occurred as momentum is building for the consolidation of a New Paradigm, driven by the diplomatic and economic policy direction defined by China's Belt-and-Road Initiative (BRI). Monumental shifts have taken place in the last months, which are moving a growing number of nations into a new strategic geometry centered around a U.S.-Russia-China alliance, which is emerging in spite of massive resistance from British and U.S. networks acting to preserve the old, dangerous world defined by geopolitics.

The goal of consolidating this new constellation of forces has been the life's work of American statesman Lyndon LaRouche, and his wife Helga Zepp-LaRouche, the founder of the Schiller Institutes, and President of the Schiller Institute in Germany, as this new geometry represents a force more powerful than that deployed by the City of London/Wall Street networks, which run the imperial forces clinging to the old, collapsing paradigm.

China and Russia worked with U.S. President Trump, along with Prime Minster Abe of Japan and South Korea's President Moon, to pull together the successful June 12 summit in Singapore between Trump and North Korea's President Kim Jong-un, which demonstrated the power of this new alliance.

The success of the Singapore summit helped pave the way for the summit between Trump and Russia's President Vladimir Putin, which will take place in Helsinki on July 16. In addition to the Trump-Kim summit, there were other events which make up parts of this picture, including the Shanghai Cooperation Organization (SCO) conference, which opened June 10 in Qingdao, China. The close collaboration between Putin and China's President Xi Jinping was a central feature of the deliberations there.

As these events proved the promise inherent in these changes, institutions of the collapsing old paradigm showed themselves to be obstacles to this new dynamic. The Toronto G-7 summit was left in a state of stunned paralysis when Trump walked out and headed for his Singapore rendezvous with Kim, after provoking its members by demanding a return of Russia to the G-8. And the European Union was left floundering, unable to patch together any positive solution to the "immigrant" crisis or to their own economic disintegration, while many EU members are now looking toward cooperation with China and the BRI as a way out of the EU's existential crisis.

These developments prompted an intervention by Mrs. LaRouche, who drafted a memo on June 17, "History Is Now Being Written in Asia: The EU Summit Must Follow the Example of Singapore." It called on EU member states to adopt the spirit of the Singapore summit, and of the organizing process which created it, to be able to overcome the ongoing failures dominating Europe. It was circulated widely, in many languages, and distributed to governments and institutions, posted on blogs. It began to shape the debate in Europe, as it offered an alternative to what Mrs. LaRouche described as barbaric proposals coming from many EU leaders.

Schiller Institute

Panel II, "How the Belt and Road Initiative Is Changing Africa: The Only Human Solution to the Refugee Crisis." From left: Wang Hao, Amzat Boukari-Yabara, H.E. Yusuf M. Tuggar, Hussein Askary, Mohammed Bila, and moderator Claudio Celani.

The approach proposed by Mrs. LaRouche was the central topic at the Schiller Institute conference, which was held outside of Frankfurt, Germany, in Bad Soden. In her keynote, she reiterated this theme in her powerful presentation which challenged participants to join with her in organizing for the New Paradigm in global strategic relations.

She opened her speech with the words, "After the very historic summit which surprised the world, between President Trump and Chairman Kim Jong-un, I made a proposal that the EU adopt this model, which shows that you can turn an adversarial relationship—as a matter of fact, we were on the verge of a potential global war—into its total opposite, into cooperation, if there is good will and if there is collaboration of the large powers, in this case, the United States, China, and Russia, which all worked in the background to help make this summit possible. So I proposed that the agenda at the just concluded EU summit should have only one point, namely the development of Africa through the New Silk Road, and that the EU should invite China's President Xi Jinping and about six or so heads of state of African nations which are already cooperating with China, to announce a joint crash program for the industrialization of Africa through the extension of the New Silk Road to all of these states."

While she acknowledged that the EU summit, which convened June 28-29, did not take up her proposal at that time, there is no alternative, she said, if Europe is to survive. This has become clear to a growing number of Europeans, who are voting in nation after nation to reject the incompetent and in some cases evil policies being put forward by their leaders, who are defending the status quo.

In the pages which follow, you will be able to read the speeches which followed that keynote, to see for yourself the quality of deliberation, and the passion of the participants for bringing about a successful transformation to the New Paradigm. Included were speakers and guests from China, Russia, the United States, Africa, and a number of countries in Europe—including Germany—who have "caught the New Silk Road Spirit," and are united in their commitment to spread it to their fellow citizens. As Mrs. LaRouche has repeatedly argued, this process will not be stopped, unless its London-centered opponents destroy the human race through genocidal wars, including possibly nuclear war. Once people grasp the beautiful idea of the potential which exists in every child, no matter how poor they may be, or where they were born, there will be an unquenchable desire to organize governments to act to protect and develop that potential.

The example of Singapore proves that such an era is now within our grasp.

Schiller Institute Conference
Bad Soden, June 30-July 1, 2018

The Urgent Need for a New Paradigm in International Relations
A Peace Order Based on the Development of Nations

SATURDAY, JUNE 30*

10:00 – CONFERENCE KEYNOTE: The Coincidence of Opposites—The World of Tomorrow
Helga Zepp-LaRouche, Chairwoman of the Schiller Institute

Panel I

How to Overcome Geopolitics and the Danger of a New World War

- Russia's Role in the New World Order
  Vladimir Morozov, Program Coordinator, Russian International Affairs Council, Moscow

- Globalization in Reverse and the Challenge for China's Foreign Policy in the New Era
  Dr. Xu Jian, Vice President of China Institute of International Studies (CIIS), Director of CIIS Academic Council, and Senior Research Fellow

- The True Interest of the United States
  U.S. State Senator Richard Black (video presentation)

- Interest Monsters: Democracy, Human Rights and Other Hypocrisies
  Lt. Col. (ret.) Ulrich Scholz, former NATO planner

The panels of day one are covered in this issue. Panels of day two will be covered in the next issue of EIR, July 13.

- The U.S. Refusal of a Multipolar World Makes the Transition Very Painful
  Colonel (ret.) Alain Corvez, International Consultant, former Counsellor for the French Defense and Interior Ministries

- The President Trump Europeans Do Not Know
  Roger Stone, U.S. Political Strategist of the Trump Faction in the Republican Party (live video presentation)

Panel II

How the Belt and Road Initiative Is Changing Africa: The Only Human Solution to the Refugee Crisis

- Opening Remarks
  Hussein Askary, Southwest Asia Coordinator of the Schiller Institute

- A Role for Europe in the Belt and Road Initiative
  Wang Hao, Embassy of the People's Republic of China to the Federal Republic of Germany, 1st Secretary for Economy and Trade

- After the Transaqua Breakthrough, Nigeria Comes to the Fore
  H.E. Yusuf Maitama Tuggar, Ambassador of the Federal Republic of Nigeria to Germany

- The Impact of Transaqua on the Future Development of Africa
  Mohammed Bila, Expert Modeler, Lake Chad Basin Observatory, Lake Chad Basin Commission

- What Pan-Africanism on the Silk Road?
  Amzat Boukari-Yabara, African Historian, General Secretary of the Pan-African League—UMOJA
- Challenges for Peace and Reconstruction in Yemen
  Representatives of the Yemeni Association Insan for Human Rights and Peace
- Operation Felix: Yemen's Reconstruction and Connection to the Belt and Road
  Hussein Askary, Southwest Asia Coordinator for the Schiller Institute

Greetings to the Conference *from Prof. Michele Geraci, newly appointed Undersecretary of State in the Ministry for Economic Development, Italy*

20:00 – CONCERT OF CLASSICAL MUSIC

Sunday, July 1

Panel III

The Future of European Nations—Cultural and Economic Grand Design within the New Paradigm

- KEYNOTE: **Europe's Future Needs to Be Inclusive, with the New Silk Roads and the World Land-Bridge**
  Jacques Cheminade, President of Solidarité et Progrès, France
- The Re-establishment of International Law
  Prof. Hans Köchler, President of Iternational Progress Organisation
- Has European Integration Gone Too Far?
  Marco Zanni, Member of the European Parliament from Italy

- The Controllable Energy
  Dr. Armin Azima, University of Hamburg

Panel IV

Economic and Political Potentials of the One Belt One Road

- How Eastern and South-Eastern Europe Can Participate in Creating a New Global Economic Miracle
  Elke Fimmen, Schiller Institute
- The New Paradigm from the View of the Balkans
  Prof. Ivo Christov, Member of Bulgarian Parliament
- The Options for Integration of the Eurasian Customs and Economic Union and China's OBOR Initiative
  Folker Hellmeyer, Economist, Germany
- On the New Silk Road—Achievements and Prospects of Economic Cooperation between Serbia and China
  Dusko Dimitrijevic, Ph.D., Professorial Fellow, Institute of International Politics and Economics, Serbia
- Necessary Regulatory Framework for Investments of German and European SME Economy in National Economies along the New Silk Road
  Hans von Helldorff, Spokesman, Federal Association of the German Silk Road Initiative
- The Eurasia Canal and the New Silk Road
  Professor Nuraly Bekturganov, Vice President of Academy of Natural Sciences of Kazakhstan
- The Integration of the Eurasian Continent
  Leonidas Chrysanthopoulos, former Ambassador of Greece, former Secretary General of the Black Sea Economic Cooperation Organization (BSEC)

18:00 – END OF CONFERENCE

The classical concert on the evening of June 30.

The Coincidence of Opposites— The World of Tomorrow

Ladies and Gentlemen, dear friends of the Schiller Institute:

After the very historic summit which surprised the world, between President Trump and Chairman Kim Jong-un, I made a proposal that this model, which shows that you can turn an adversarial relationship—as a matter of fact, we were on the verge of a potential global war—into the total opposite of cooperation if there is good will and if there is collaboration of the large powers—in this case, the United States, China, and Russia, who all worked in the background to help make this summit possible.

Helga Zepp-LaRouche, founder of the Schiller Institutes.

I proposed that at the EU summit, which has just concluded, the agenda should have only one item, namely the development of Africa through the New Silk Road. And that the EU should invite President Xi Jinping and about six or so heads of state of African nations which are already cooperating with China, and announce a joint crash program for the industrialization of Africa through the extension of the New Silk Road to all of these states.

Such action, if taken, would have had absolute credibility and would have been taken seriously through the presence of President Xi Jinping, because he has a very high reputation in Africa; it would have given hope to all the young people of Africa, that they might have a prospect of participating in the construction of their own countries, and building up their nations. For Europe, this is the only human way to solve the refugee crisis.

This proposal has been translated into ten languages or more: most European languages, Russian, Chinese, Japanese, Korean, and is being circulated widely internationally. Did I think that this was a realistic program for this EU? Well, absolutely not. But, is it the right idea to be pushed anyway? Yes. After all, such a summit could be called at any moment by any combination of nations. One could use the UN General Assembly in September to discuss this.

Trump-Putin Summit

A new summit has been confirmed in the meantime between President Putin and President Trump for the 16th of July, in Helsinki, after the NATO summit. They will probably discuss a U.S.-Russian agreement on the future of Syria; maybe even a comprehensive plan for Southwest Asia. And secondly, there will be discussion about the need to have global nuclear disarmament, which was announced by Russian Ambassador to the United States, Anatoly Antonov. At the same time however, President Putin made clear that he is calling for global denuclearization from a position of strength; he gave a press conference at the Kremlin the same day, saying that there are a number of Russian weapons systems, where Russia is years, if not decades, ahead of the West. This was what he announced on March 1st. In the meantime, Generals Dunford and Gerasimov met in Helsinki to prepare this summit.

The neo-liberal establishment of the West went absolutely out of their minds. They basically freaked out and called this an "apocalyptic development"—that was *Die Welt* and the London *Times*—especially being completely freaked out about the possibility that Trump may reduce the U.S. troops in Europe, which obviously would be a good thing. But the geopolitical faction went absolutely out of control over this possibility.

This abreaction of the West to something which any peace-loving person could only welcome, namely that the relationship between the large powers—China, the United States, and Russia—would be improved, proves that something else is needed. We need a completely New Paradigm in thinking in terms of the relations among nations.

Syrian refugees cross the border from Hungary to Austria, on their way to Germany in 2015.

The Refugee Crisis

Coming back to the refugee crisis: The annual global trend report of the UN Refugee Agency published that by the end of 2017, there were 68.5 million people displaced on the Earth. This is almost the size of the German population; 16.2 million new refugees in 2017; 44,500 new refugees every day, or 1 person every 2 seconds. We should keep in mind that each of these individuals is as human a person as you and me and all of us in this room. These are not numbers; these are people like your neighbor, like your friend, your family.

The EU just concluded, proposing a whole number of vague things: "disembarkment camps," militarize the European Border and Coast Guard Agency (Frontex), and similar things which are as barbarian as they are unworkable. They want to close the outer borders of the EU; make Frontex a robust mandate; spend a lot of money. European Parliament President Antonio Tajani proposed EU6 billion to close the Mediterranean across the coast of Libya alone. Ex-NATO Gen. Egon Romms even demanded a Bundeswehr mandate to back up Frontex, and others called for NATO to be involved.

"Disembarkment" centers are supposed to set on European soil, later in Africa; but the problem is, none of the countries involved want them. Not Egypt, not Libya, not Morocco, not Tunisia, not Algeria; and the Albanians and Macedonians don't want to have them either. Libya proposes such camps to be set up south of the Libyan borders, in Niger and Mali, which have zero infrastructure, just desert.

German TV reported that the Algerian government sent 13,000 refugees into the Sahara without food and water, without cell phones or money. In a heat of 48° Celsius [118° Fahrenheit], people had to march to some little village in Niger. Pregnant women and children, many of them were never seen again. The Algerian government denied that this was true. It may be true or not—one never knows in the world of fake news. But I can assure you that this is happening all the time; people are marching through the Sahara, dying, and it is not being reported. Pope Francis compared these camps in Libya for example, where there is not even a government in control, where people have been tortured, mutilated, raped, sold as slaves, to the concentration camps of the Second World War set up by the Nazis.

States have the right to protect their borders, to keep social peace. But you cannot ignore the right to life, the right for asylum, and the plight of the refugees. The Prime Minister of Albania, Edi Rama, said Albania will never allow these camps; he is against dumping desperate people like toxic waste nobody wants, and that Albania will never be a wave breaker for the refugees. If you look at the refugee debate in Europe at this point— and we have had a lot of it in the last days—where are the Western values of human rights and democracy? What we are seeing with the refugee crisis is the *violation* of the most basic human rights: the right to life, dignity, asylum, before the eyes of the world public.

A Fundamental Change in the Image of Man

Underneath all the brutality is a fundamental change in the image of man, what Russian Foreign Minister Lavrov called "post-Christian values," which reflect a complete deadening of compassion, a complete loss of respect for the sacredness of the human life. Some of the worst hardliners of the so-called Christian parties talk about "asylum tourists" or "refugee shuttle boats," which reflects a pathological indifference to the suffering and dying of human beings.

After the Second World War, the Federal Republic of Germany's first Chancellor, Konrad Adenauer, explicitly wanted to create the Christian Democratic Union (CDU) as a Christian party with Christian values as a bulwark, so that the atrocities of National Socialism would never happen again. Now, *Der Spiegel* talks about "fascism" with respect to President Trump; but his policies are no different than those of the European Union. So, how did this happen? We have to go back to the paradigm shift which occurred in the West. Step by step, we moved away from what Adenauer meant, to a zero-growth ideology—pushed by the Club of Rome, by the World Wildlife Fund, by the ecology movement—that we are in a world of limited resources in a closed system, where every human being is a burden to nature.

This was then escalated by the complete deregulation of the markets, the increase of power of the Wall Street and the City of London, the complete dominance of the neo-liberal dogma that the markets are the supreme authority which have replaced God. The role of the state is no longer to protect the common good, but to guarantee the rights of the banks and the speculators, which we saw especially after 2008, with the complete deregulation of the financial system. It became like a self-service shop for the rich at the expense of the majority of the population; austerity against the common good; privatization of all categories of life and the economy; and a devastating increase in wealth disparity.

The image of man has been subject to a cost-benefit analysis; the idea that there is no knowable truth, but just post-factual opinion, where the entire reality is subjugated to the economic model of competition. Even democracy has to be in conformity with the markets. This is the famous sentence by German Chancellor Angela Merkel: we live in a democracy, but it has to conform to the markets. After the recent election in Italy, EU Commissioner Oettinger said, because they didn't like the Lega and the Five Star Movement having won the election, "The markets will teach the Italians how to vote." This shows the complete arrogance of the neo-liberal establishment. They are completely unable to recognize the causes of the decline of the Western model. This decline is not the fault of China or Putin, it is entirely caused by the policies of the West.

LaRouche Development Proposals

When the Soviet Union allowed the peaceful reunification of Germany in 1989-90, there was a possibility to go in a completely different direction. After the disintegration of the Soviet Union, there was the chance for a peace order for the 21st Century, because one bloc had dissolved, and there was no more enemy. In 1988, my husband Lyndon LaRouche, having foresight that the Wall was coming down soon, proposed the soon-to-happen reunification of Germany with Berlin as its capital, and that the development of Poland become a model for the entire Comecon, working with Western technologies. After the collapse of the Soviet Union, we proposed to extend the Paris-Berlin-Vienna Productive Triangle concept to all of Eurasia, calling it the Eurasian Land-Bridge, which is what the New Silk Road is becoming today.

Earlier, Lyndon LaRouche had proposed an International Development Bank in 1975; an Oasis Development Plan for Southwest Asia; he worked with López Portillo on a Latin American integration proposal called Operation Juárez. We worked with India's Prime Minister Indira Gandhi on a 40-year plan for India; we worked on a 50-year Pacific Basin development plan. My husband was the author of the Strategic Defense Initiative—which was quite different than the media represented it—it involved a gigantic technology transfer to the developing sector. If the life's work of Lyndon LaRouche had been accepted by the neo-liberal establishment, I can assure you, Africa today would be a blossoming continent, and the world would look very different.

After the collapse of the Soviet Union, they said "OK, now communism has been defeated, let's have a unipolar world; a Project for a New American Century. Let's implement shock therapy on Russia. Let's get rid of all governments that oppose us through regime change, color revolution. Let's repeal Glass-Steagall. Let's have 'humanitarian' interventionist wars based on lies." We see the result of such policies in the refugee crisis in the Middle East, and the impoverishment of the developing sector, and southern Europe, for that matter.

This is the policy of the last 20-30 years of the West. And the result is, the Western system is collapsing. You have a revolt from within—Brexit; Trump's election; the Austrian election; the rebellion in the Central and East European states. Therefore, to have the kind of Merkel solution to all of these problems is completely out of the way.

We will see what happens, because the result of the just-concluded European Union summit is very vague; everything is voluntary, a lot of bilateral negotiations will happen. And we have to see if CSU leader Seehofer finds this acceptable, because he said ahead of the summit, that if the CSU capitulates to Merkel, they could start singing the *Requiem*. That is a good thing, because if the CSU starts to sing Classical music, that would be a big improvement right there; but he meant it with respect to the upcoming Bavarian state election.

So, there may be an effort to patch things up. But it

Xinhua

Chinese President Xi Jinping and world leaders at the Belt and Road Forum for International Cooperation, Beijing, May 14, 2017.

will not work, because there is still the danger of a new financial crash; all the indicators are about 40% worse than in 2008. The debt level, especially the corporate debt level, the Level 3 derivatives of the banks are all about 40% worse. The danger therefore is a collapse into chaos. A few days ago, the defense ministers of nine EU countries decided to create a European military intervention force to deal with crises around the world—now that's pretty pretentious if they can't even get the EU together to have such an approach. But all of this shows, from the EU and from the West in general, that no positive initiatives are forthcoming to address the strategic problems in the world.

The New Silk Road is Changing Everything

However, there is a completely different model and perspective in play. Almost five years ago, President Xi Jinping put the New Silk Road on the agenda as a revival of the ancient Silk Road, which was an exchange of goods, cultures, and technologies, improving the lives of all participating countries. In the meantime, the New Silk Road, or the Belt and Road Initiative (BRI) as it's called, has become the largest infrastructure project in the world. According to China's Foreign Minister Wang Yi, the BRI already involves 140 countries working together on a win-win basis. They are realizing six major corridors in Eurasia; hundreds of projects—rail lines, industry parks, hydropower—in Africa, Latin America, and Asia.

But the BRI is not just an economic program. President Xi calls it a "community of a shared future for mankind." It's a completely new model of relations among nations working together on a win-win perspective; respect for national sovereignty; non-interference into the internal affairs—a completely different system. At the

19th National Congress of the Communist Party of China, Xi Jinping proposed a vision for the next 35 years, which is unparalleled in the world: By 2020, China will eliminate all poverty within its borders. And given the fact that China has already gotten 700 million people out of poverty and they are now engaged in a gigantic program to address each single household still living in poverty, you can be absolutely certain that they will succeed.

By 2025, China wants to be leading in several areas of science and technology. By 2035, China is supposed to be a fully modernized socialist country; and by 2050, a large modern socialist country—blossoming, strong, democratic, culturally advanced, harmonious, and beautiful, where wealth will be available for everybody. The Chinese will live a happier and safer life, and be a full, active member of the world community. There is also a total obligation for all Party members to devote themselves to the common good, to have the highest moral standards, work with a full heart for the improvement of conditions of the life of the entire population.

Xi Jinping invoked China's rich cultural tradition of 5,000 years and the essential contributions China has made to the universal development of mankind, calling this the great Chinese dream, whose contributions ensure that all of humanity will live a happier life in a beautiful world. China's economy is based on innovation; the political system is based on meritocracy; but it's not just for China, because China is now offering the most advanced technologies to the developing countries, especially in the area of nuclear energy and cooperation in space research and development.

Now this new Chinese model, the New Silk Road model, is very attractive. After centuries of colonialism, and the infamous IMF and World Bank conditionalities,

China is providing cheap credit and even grants to Africa and other developing areas. For the first time, many countries in Africa, Latin America, and Asia are hopeful—about overcoming poverty and underdevelopment, and having productive and fulfilling jobs for their young people.

The various Western think tanks, which completely arrogantly ignored the progress of the New Silk Road for about four years, all of a sudden have woken up to discover this incredible dynamic underway. Suddenly a flurry of furious reports were written claiming that China has ulterior motives, that China has an authoritarian character. If you ask people in the developing sector about that, however, that is exactly not what they think. They think China is giving them hope for the first time. The problem is that the neo-liberal elites see the world through geopolitical glasses, and they project their own intention: Since their own policies are neo-colonial, they cannot imagine that there is a country on this planet devoted to the common good of the entire world population.

Schiller Institute

Helga Zepp-LaRouche and Lyndon LaRouche.

Confucius and Nicholas of Cusa and Lyndon LaRouche

When China speaks about "Socialism with Chinese characteristics," I personally believe this essentially refers to the Confucianism, which was the dominant philosophy in China for 2,500 years, with the exception of ten years of the Cultural Revolution. Confucius is absolutely important to be studied, because he has an image of man which is very close to the humanism we used to have in Europe. It's the idea of lifelong learning, that every person has the potential to become a *junzi,* which means basically a sage, which is exactly the same idea as the beautiful soul of Friedrich Schiller. If you develop yourself through lifelong learning, there can be harmony in the family. If all members can realize all their potentials, this then allows for harmony in the state and harmony among the states.

The geopolitical establishment and most ordinary citizens in the West are completely unable to think in the win-win concept based on Confucian philosophy, because they are so used to thinking in terms of a zero-sum game—one wins, the other loses. The one great Western philosopher who is the best pedagogue to teach you to think in a different way, is Nicholas of Cusa with his conception of the *coincidentia oppositorum;* the coincidence of opposites. He is not known in China; I

found only one professor there who is in charge of comparative religions, but Nicholas of Cusa was not just a religious man. He was the founder of the modern scientific method, of the sovereign nation-state, of the representative system, and even if many of his arguments are derived from the theological realm, they are still of tremendous philosophical and scientific importance.

On the way back from Constantinople in 1437-38, where he had brought the delegation of the Greek Orthodox Church to the Councils of Ferrara and Florence, he said that all of sudden he had had an inspiration which enabled him to see all questions in a completely different light; namely, the coincidence of opposites; which was an idea against Aristotle, who basically had argued that contradictory statements cannot be at the same time true. Cusa said this has been the common axiom of philosophy so far, and Aristotle was just the most explicit in expressing this. Then he quotes Philo of Alexandria saying that the logic of Aristotelian thinking is not on a higher level than the *ratio* of the animals.

In a very important writing called *Apologia de Docta Ignorantia* [In Defense of Learned Ignorance], which was a rebuttal to a scholastic scholar named Wenck, Cusa explains why Aristotle is an inferior thinker, only capable of a methodological back and forth. In *De Docta Ignorantia*, he says "The coincidence of opposite thinking is like being on a high tower, where the one who oversees everything, sees the process in its totality. The seeker, the searched, the process of searching, also how the searcher gets closer or further away from the searched." In another writing called *De Visione Dei* [On the Vision of God], he develops a pedagogy for training the mind to think in terms of the *coincidentia oppositorum* to overcome a mental wall behind which you have the level of reason.

In *De Docta Ignorantia*, Nicholas also speaks of the *spiritus universorum* which unites religions, nations, peoples, which are elements of differentiation, but that the universe as a whole is the perfect expression for the precondition for everything to exist. *Quodlibet in quolibet* is a very famous sentence by Nicholas: "Everything participates in all." For the political order, that means the multiplicity of people can be integrated without violating their specific identity, because of the totality of the order which already exists. According to Nicholas, each human being is a microcosm, which contains in germ form the entire macrocosm in a complex, unextended way, which is very much like the monad concept of Leibniz. Harmony, according to this philosophy, a peace order, is only possible if all microcosms develop in the best possible way, that the development of the other is the reciprocal self-interest of each for the harmony to function.

If one wants to find a solution to the political problems of today, one has to think in terms of this *coincidentia oppositorum*; to think in terms of the common aims of mankind first, that the one has a higher order than the magnitude of the many. Therefore, self-perfection and ennoblement require an increase in the potential relative population density as a precondition for the existence of future generations.

My husband Lyndon LaRouche has proven in numerous writings why an increase in the potential relative population density and the continuous increase in [our technological] energy flux-density is mandatory. At each given level of technology, a civilization eventually reaches a point of exhaustion in terms of resources and costs. To head off such disaster requires continued, qualitative breakthroughs in the knowledge of the physical principles of the universe, the continuing higher division of labor, and more and more creative minds to participate in the limitless progress of humanity.

Today, this *spiritus universorum* idea exists in the form of the New Silk Road spirit. A community of nations, as the basis for the common good of all, is the only way to address the problems of today. This spirit is now being felt in Asia, Latin America, and Africa, and in more and more countries in Europe. Nicholas of Cusa, in a sermon on the Feast of Epiphany in 1456 in Brixen, which was called by commentators a "Hymn to Civilization," praised the arts and natural sciences as the great gift to mankind in which all must participate, so as not to slow the development of one single human being. And that is exactly what the New Silk Road is doing.

The New Silk Road Spirit made possible the Singapore summit. Meetings are now taking place where the building of railroads on the western and soon eastern coast of North Korea, uniting South Korea and North Korea with the Chinese transport corridors and the Trans-Siberian Railroad, is being discussed and planned. President Trump promised that North Korea will soon be a prosperous country. China and Russia also said that they plan to play a big role in this. *Global Times*, the English-language Chinese newspaper, said "The geographical location of North Korea makes it predestined for the integration into the Belt and Road Initiative," and that this would happen much sooner than anybody could imagine.

We propose to take the same approach to Africa. Instead of the militarization of the refugee policy, have a New Silk Road plan. If the EU is willing to spend tens of billions on camps, on fortification of Europe, let's set up, instead, credit lines for the industrialization, basic economic infrastructure, water projects such as huge projects like Transaqua, mass transport, fast train rails, maglev, health care facilities, educational systems, space-oriented science-driver programs, new cities based on modular urban development. If all European nations would join together with China, India, Japan, and also the United States, and announce their common commitment to such a policy and projects, and do so with the cooperation of the African states who want to be part of such a crash program, the refugee crisis could be turned around.

But this approach requires a passionate love for humanity—exactly as Ethiopia's Prime Minister Abiy Ahmed Ali recently told a mass rally of half a million people shortly before there was an assassination attempt against him—he said, "The only way to move forward from all this history is forgiveness and love. Revenge is for the weak. And because Ethiopians are not weak, we won't need revenge. We will win with love."

So, let us act likewise. The world is in an incredible turmoil. It's very complex, and I do not believe the problems will be solved by having a zillion partial solutions. We need a higher level of reason that will unite all of humanity. I think we have reached the end of an epoch, the end of geopolitics. And we must reach the New Paradigm where we think in terms of the coincidence of opposites; what Xi Jinping has called a "community for a shared future of humanity." If Europe is willing to survive, we will organize the European countries to join this effort.

How to Overcome Geopolitics and the Danger of a New World War

VLADIMIR MOROZOV

Russia's Role in the New World Order

Vladimir Morozov is the Program Coordinator, Russian International Affairs Council, Moscow.

Dear Ladies and Gentlemen:

First of all allow me to thank the Schiller Institute and Mrs. Zepp-LaRouche personally for this great opportunity of being here today with all of you, and discussing with the interesting and esteemed guests the future of the global world order and the role different countries and regions may play in it.

I'll also share with you the idea that with the current political and economic dynamics, both on global,

Vladimir Morozov

regional and national scales, it's high time we openly discuss the future of international relations and principles that should guide the interaction between states and regions.

Unipolar, Multipolar, Multilateral

Let us look at some key ideas. First, even though we assumed a unipolar world with an absolute dominance of one superpower, is about to end soon, there is no alternative so far that is clear and feasible, and that is within our reach. A multipolar world, which has long been advocated by many countries, can be no better alternative.

Secondly, Russia's role in the new global order will be determined more by its domestic dynamics, rather than the composition of the world order. However, Russia will play an important part in all the different regions, and possibly globally, trying not only to stabilize its immediate neighborhood, but also serving as one of the interconnectors in Eurasia and one of the guarantors of global security and stability. Thirdly—and I guess this is one of the crucial points—we cannot change the global order overnight. If we want an evolutionary, rather than a revolutionary change which will imply a global war, we first need to concentrate on rebuilding trust. But trust is also something that we cannot rebuild overnight.

It is widely assumed that the only alternative to the present status quo, is a multipolar world. When we talk about the future of the global order, nearly everyone, in Russia—in Europe, in China, in the Middle East—agrees that the desired world order should be multipolar. But the idea of multipolarity traces back to the 1970s, with the rise of the Asia-Pacific countries, with the creation of the Trilateral Commission, etc. These ideas were extremely popular during the mid-1990s. However, our world is still not, in essence, multipolar. And what is more, when discussing polarity—multipolarity, unipolarity—people tend to get confused on the definition of polarity.

Multipolarity is, in fact, another version of the Congress of Vienna (November 1814 to June 1815)—a world order dominated by the balance of power and divided by several power centers, competing for the limited global resources. Although such an order is based on the interests of more than one state, it never takes into account the interests of smaller states, and those states that are not part of the global equilibrium, are disregarded by the global players. In a way, this kind of order will be a comeback of geopolitics, the thing we all try to avoid when discussing the future of the global order.

But what can the alternative to a unipolar or a multipolar world order be? There is a growing debate in Russia about this. Recently, we have published a new article by our director general, proposing that an alternative to multipolarity can be multilateralism. He says that multilateralism can be the best alternative that prevents the world from sliding down into confrontation and, thus, world war.

The key difference between multipolarity and multilateralism, is that multilateralism is based on the balance of *interests* rather than balance of *power*. It is insufficient for such an order to be based solely on the existing structures of the West, like NATO, the European Union, NAFTA, etc.; It must also incorporate the UN, the G20, the OECD, the Shanghai Cooperation Organization, the Asia-Pacific Economic Cooperation (APEC); and possibly—possibly—we can come to a sort of collective security system for the Middle East and Africa.

However, we should take into account that what Donald Trump is doing is a symptom of an institutional fatigue, not only in the West but also in the East, and therefore, if we want to slide to a multilateral world, we need to concentrate not only on the institutions but also on the regimes, international regimes, and first and foremost, on nuclear non-proliferation and development assistance.

Russia's Role

Talking about Russia's role in the new global order, I guess that Russia's role will, as I said, be largely determined by its domestic dynamics. Putin has entered his last term in power, and now he's likely to concentrate more on the domestic agenda than on the international one. This means maintaining several major economic reforms, dealing with pensions, with the economic output, etc., and of course, the issue of power transition and political stability after 2024.

This, however, doesn't mean that Russia will be leaving the global stage. We have to not be involved in all the matters the world offers to us, but what is crucial about the Russian foreign policy and Russia's position in the world, is that Russia's top foreign policy priority is internal and external security. This means that Russia is not willing, as it is constantly accused of by the West, to destabilize the regions bordering Russia, but is ready to use its military power and even project it overseas, as in the case of the Middle East in Syria, to help foster

Russian President Vladimir Putin (left) with President of China Xi Jinping at the 2016 Shanghai Cooperation Organisation (SCO) Summit.

stability and help foster the national interests of the country.

This is how Russia remarkably differs from the EU and China, neither of which is involved in military operations overseas, but also from the U.S., which constantly interferes in global affairs, practically for short-term interests.

Secondly, while Russia is interested in stabilizing its bordering regions, especially the common neighborhood of the European Union and Russia, between Russia and China, etc., Russia will place more emphasis on the Chinese Belt and Road Initiative. For Russia, the Belt and Road Initiative is not only an economic project which fosters Russia's position as one of the transport hubs and interconnectors in Eurasia, but is also a way of stabilizing its most dangerous neighborhood, involving the Central Asia countries and Afghanistan, which can possibly explode if we do not stop extremism spreading there, and if we do not provide the people living there with a suitable economic alternative to raising drugs and terrorism. This is why Russia will continue its cooperation with China, especially with the co-development initiative President Putin and President Xi Jinping agreed to, concerning the co-development of the Eurasian Economic Union and the Belt and Road Initiative.

Also, when talking about Russia's foreign policy identity, I'm rather skeptical about the idea of "Eurasianism" in Russian foreign policy. I personally prefer the term "Euro-Pacific" power—in which we assume that Russia is a European country. But Russia has access to the Pacific region; it will be involved in all the matters, all the problems, all the conflicts that will go on in the Pacific region; and Russia can also serve as one of the parties interested in resolving these conflicts, especially the North Korea case and having access to the Asia Pacific gives Russia special relations not only with China, but also with the Republic of Korea and Japan, and also with the United States.

We can anticipate further Russian engagement in Syria, especially after the situation is stabilized and the terrorism is defeated. What Russia constantly proposes, apart from the postwar reconstruction of Syria, involving the European Union, the United States, of course, China, is creating a collective security system for the Middle East. This should also include not only Syria, but also Israel, Saudi Arabia, Iran, China, the United States, and the European Union and Russia, of course— as the guarantors that longstanding peace comes to the region.

I like the idea of the Eurasian Land-Bridge, but it's not only about the infrastructural project building rapid train lines from Germany to Moscow. It is also about people-to-people contacts. When we still have the visa regimes between the European Union and Russia, it really impedes the human, people-to-people contacts, and exchange of cultures, exchange of ideas, and exchange of opportunities.

The Trump-Putin Summit—What to Expect

Last but not least, as we all understand, the global order cannot be changed overnight. We can still propose some quick fixes in the meantime that would help stabilize Russia-Western and especially Russia-U.S. relations. First and foremost, I guess that many people here are very much looking forward to the upcoming Trump-Putin summit in Helsinki in July, but I guess not as much as they looked forward to the Trump-Kim Jong-un summit—but still. I think we should not anticipate, much, these talks, especially because the two countries are coming in with an explicit roadmap of restoring the bilateral relations and getting Russia-West relations back on track.

But still, I think that if this summit happens, it will be a major breakthrough from the past four to five years, because I guess the last such summit was held six years ago in 2012, between Obama and Medvedev. The Putin-Trump talks can create an atmosphere of trust and cooperation that may help restore relations. This is also true with regard to the possibility of an upcoming visit of representatives of the U.S. Congress to Russia.

Meanwhile, Some Quick Fixes

What could be the possible quick fixes? Firstly, we need to restore the diplomatic representation of the United States in Russia and that of Russia in the United States. Expelling diplomats not only severely affected the political dialogue, but also people-to-people contacts—getting visas for Russian citizens to visit the United States now takes up to half a year or a year, and I guess the same is true for U.S. citizens wishing to visit Russia.

Once we have a political dialogue going, the most urgent issue the two Presidents should discuss, is maintaining the strategic stability. This includes not only the new START Treaty, its possible extension, and all further nuclear disarmament, but also the future of the Intermediate-Range Nuclear Forces (INF) Treaty. Preserving the latter is vital for European security, and soon—as we want to avoid an ever-greater arms race and its possible, unprecedented escalation. We need an open dialogue between not only our politicians, but also our technical specialists, including the military, on the problems we have in implementing these treaties and what other actions we can take in order to resolve our differences.

The next steps will be, of course, talks on Syria to stabilize that country, and of course, taking control away from the terrorists and restoring it to the legitimate government; and also dealing with the Ukrainian problem. However, I'm not expecting that much will be done in the meantime regarding Ukraine, but still, if we have an atmosphere of trust and if we have an atmosphere of cooperation, we will be able to resolve it.

Once again, thank you so much for your attention, and I'm looking forward to your questions.

DR. XU JIAN

Globalization in Reverse and the Challenge for China's Foreign Policy in the New Era

Dr. Xu Jian is Vice President of the China Institute of International Studies (CIIS), Director of the CIIS Academic Council, and Senior Research Fellow. This is his edited speech as received for delivery on Panel 1, June 30, 2018.

President Helga Zepp-LaRouche, distinguished guests, ladies and gentlemen:

It is my great honor to be invited to attend the conference held in such a beautiful place. Today, I will briefly talks about globalization in reverse, China's foreign policy, and the challenges facing China, including the three traps. There are some misconceptions and misjudgments by Western countries toward China's development, which hinder the relations between China and the West. Our host, the Schiller Institute, offers me an opportunity here to explain China's policies and China's initiatives to resolve misunderstandings toward China.

I. China's Perception of Globalization in Reverse

The trend of globalization in reverse is a hot issue in the current international landscape and it has been especially prominent in Western developed countries. Brexit, Donald Trump's election as President of the United States, and the tremendous impact of far right forces on the political ecology of France, Germany, Italy and other major European countries, have reflected the rampant backlash against globalization in Western countries from different angles. In some developing countries, protectionism and nationalism have also emerged to varying degrees in recent years, which shows the trends of reverse globalization, anti-global-

Dr. Xu Jian

ization and deglobalization are not limited to the developed world, but are a worldwide phenomenon with varying forms and momentum in different countries and regions.

Globalization in reverse and global trade protectionism are not accidental phenomena; there is a deep background for their rise and they are closely related to some problems of globalization, the most prominent of which is the inequality of social distribution and the uneven development among nations. Unequal social distribution is a weakness inherent in market economy, but economic globalization further exacerbates the problem. In market economy, the profit of different economic factors varies significantly, among which the difference between capital and other factors of production is most outstanding. The findings of French economist Thomas Piketty in this regard deserve special attention. Piketty believes that if the return on capital is much higher than the economic growth rate over a relatively long period, the risk of wealth distribution differentiation will become considerable.

The problem of uneven development among countries that arises from the process of globalization is equally profound and complex, which has two manifestations: the North-South problem and the East-West problem. For the North-South problem, globalization has not only spawned a group of emerging economies that contribute to the collective rising of developing countries, but has also marginalized a number of others. Such countries not only have limited benefits from globalization, but are also facing increasing risks and pressures. As a result, the gap between them on one hand, and the developed and even emerging countries on the other, is widening further. This situation has exacerbated the political and social ecology within these countries and is also one of the key factors in some continued regional conflicts and unrest.

There are complicated reasons for the marginalization of some countries in globalization, both domestically and internationally. On the international front, the biased rules of globalization have forged an international competitive environment that is detrimental to the well-being of these countries. Until recently, globalization has been dominated by developed countries, and relevant rules have accommodated their interests. This situation has improved considerably since the beginning of the 21st Century, with the efforts of developing countries, but there are still many unjust factors in the international order, and the North-South contradiction remains a prominent problem in the development of globalization.

The East-West imbalance mainly manifests itself between emerging and developed economies. The inexorable rise of a large number of developing countries over the past twenty or thirty years, especially major emerging countries, has changed the dominance of Western developed countries in the international balance of power. The world architecture is undergoing changes, changes without precedent in the last centuries, that strongly boost the development of multi-polarization. The uneven development has important positive effects on the progress of human society. However, as the world economy is under downward pressure, such a trend has also worsened the contradiction between developed and emerging countries in the international order. Particularly after the international financial crisis, Western developed countries, including the United States and European countries, have been confronted with many development dilemmas, and the contradictions between developed and emerging countries have also become more prominent.

Developed countries' accusation against the emerging countries of free-riding reflects their intention to justify their own problems, but also has bearing on the difficulties of developing countries in enforcing the rules. It is needless to say that fair play depends not only on the fairness of the rules themselves, but also on whether the fair rules are observed, as well as on the effect of the implementation. As the economic volume of emerging countries grows, the difference in effects of implementing the rules has been increasingly relevant to the international competition and the order of globalization.

To conclude, the current reverse of globalization is the result of various kinds of problems regarding justice and uneven development in the process of globalization. The reasons for these problems are complicated, involving almost all participants in globalization. The resolution of these problems is not a unilateral responsibility of a particular category of countries, but a common obligation of all participants in globalization.

With regard to the development of globalization, we should transcend the limitation of narrow nationalism and understand it with the idea of the community of shared future for mankind. In his remarks at the General Debate of the 70th session of the UN General Assembly in 2015, President Xi Jinping said: "The greatest ideal is to create a world truly shared by all." Peace, development, equity, justice, democracy and freedom are common values of all mankind and the lofty goals of the United Nations. Yet these goals are far from being achieved, and we must continue our endeavor to meet them." To uphold and promote the universal values of all mankind, advance the community of shared future, and promote the common welfare of all people should be the guiding beliefs of shaping the new globalization.

We need to inject new impetus into globalization through new initiatives. In this regard, China's Belt and Road Initiative has outstanding significance. The Belt and Road mobilizes both international and domestic resources, coordinates the two civilizations of land and sea, and champions the vision of shared, mutually beneficial and balanced development, providing convenience and conditions for the people along the routes to create value and injecting new impetus into the transformation of globalization.

Certainly the transformation of globalization needs more new driving forces like the Belt and Road Initiative. With concerted efforts, countries can also forge more open channels for cooperation at international, regional and bilateral levels, such as the exploration and construction of the Regional Comprehensive Economic Partnership (RCEP), the Asia-Pacific FTA (FTAAP) and the China-Japan-South Korea FTA, and the promotion of agreements in investment and other areas between China and the United States, and China and Europe, so as to provide more positive energy for globalization.

II. China's Foreign Policy in the New Era

In the 19th National Congress of the Communist Party of China (CPC), Xi Jinping summarized China's world views by arguing that "the world is undergoing major developments, transformation, and adjustment, but peace and development remain the call of our day." In this process, Xi emphasized: "Our world is full of both hope and challenges." On the one hand, the "trends of global multi-polarity, economic globalization, IT application, and cultural diversity are surging forward; changes in the global governance system and the international order are speeding up; countries are becoming increasingly interconnected and interdependent; relative international forces are becoming more balanced; and peace and development remain irreversible trends." On the other hand, however, "as a world we face growing uncertainties and destabilizing factors. Global economic growth lacks energy; the gap between rich and poor continues to widen; hotspot issues arise often in some regions; and unconventional security threats like terrorism, cyber-insecurity, major infectious diseases, and climate change continue to spread. As human beings we have many common challenges to face."

Against this background, Xi warned that "no country can address alone the many challenges facing mankind; no country can afford to retreat into self-isolation." At the same time, he expressed a relatively positive attitude towards the prospects of the world by calling that "we should not give up on our dreams because the reality around us is too complicated; we should not stop pursuing our ideals because they seem out of our reach."

Xi's summary of China's world outlook in the political report delivered at the 19th National Congress of the CPC comprehensively reflects the mainstream views of China on the situation of the world. From the academic point of view, Xi's evaluation of both opportunities and challenges facing the current world is well-balanced, with a question-orientation and an optimistic tone.

There are two central pillars in terms of the framework of China's foreign policy: The first one is "to build a community with a shared future for mankind, to build an open, inclusive, clean, and beautiful world that enjoys lasting peace, universal security, and common prosperity." The second one is to "forge a new form of international relations featuring mutual respect, fairness, justice, and win-win cooperation."

The basic approach of China's foreign policy is to develop global partnerships and expand the convergence of interests with other countries. With this approach, "China will promote coordination and cooperation with other major countries and work to build a framework for major country relations featuring overall stability and balanced development. China will deepen relations with its neighbors in accordance with the principle of amity, sincerity, mutual benefit, and inclusiveness, and the policy of forging friendship and partnership with its neighbors. China will—guided by the principle of upholding justice while pursuing shared interests and the principle of sincerity, real results, affinity, and good faith—work to strengthen solidarity and cooperation with other developing countries."

III. China's Challenge: Properly Handling Three Traps

China is now facing some challenges, including how to cope with the "Thucydides Trap," the "Kindleberger Trap," and the Cold War Trap.

The first challenge China now encounters is how to cope with a paradox between two related traps. The paradox was first pointed out by Joseph S. Nye, Professor of Harvard University, although it was referred to as a problem faced by the United States. Nye argued in an article immediately after Donald Trump came to power: "As U.S. President-elect Donald Trump prepares his administration's policy toward China, he should be wary of two major traps that history has set for him." One is the "Thucydides Trap," which refers to the warning by the ancient Greek historian that cataclysmic war can erupt if an established power (like the United States) becomes too fearful of a rising power (like China). "But Trump also has to worry about the "Kindleberger Trap."

According to Professor Nye: "Charles Kindleberger, an intellectual architect of the Marshall Plan who later taught at MIT, argued that the disastrous decade of the 1930s was caused when the U.S. replaced Britain as the largest global power but failed to take on Britain's role in providing global public goods. The result was the collapse of the global system into depression, genocide, and world war."

The most interesting point of Nye's argument lies with a dilemma the United States may face when it tries to cope with the two traps. On the one hand, according to Nye, the main problem of the Thucydides Trap for the United States comes mainly from "a China that seems too strong rather than too weak." On the other hand, the problem of the Kindleberger Trap may emerge because of "a China that seems too weak rather than too strong" to help provide global public goods. President Trump is therefore facing a paradox, if only because he "must worry about a China that is simultaneously too weak and too strong. To achieve his objectives, he must avoid the Kindleberger trap as well as the Thucydides trap. But, above all, he must avoid the miscalculations, misperceptions, and rash judgments that plague human history." (Joseph S. Nye, "The Kindleberger Trap," March 1, 2017, Project Syndicate)

Unfortunately, the paradox faced by the United States seems to apply more or less to China as well. In a period when the Trump Administration pursues the "putting America first" strategy and prepares to reduce the United States' contribution to providing international public goods, the pressure of the Kindleberger Trap on China grows inevitably. If China refuses or hesitates to take more responsibilities in providing global public goods, it is almost certain to hear stronger criticism that China continues to free-ride rather than contribute to the existing international order. If China does the opposite, that is, to take more international responsibilities which fit in with China's rapidly growing national strength, as it has done, it is also unavoidable to hear the accusation that China is in search of regional and even global hegemony.

Reading the accusation about China made in the National Security Strategy of the United States of America delivered in December 2017 helps understand how serious the dilemma faced by China may become. This document, referred to by President Trump as "an America First National Security Strategy," argues that the increasing competitions in the world "require the United States to rethink the policies of the past two decades— policies based on the assumption that engagement with rivals and their inclusion in international institutions and global commerce would turn them into benign actors and trustworthy partners." It concludes: "For the most part, this premise turned out to be false." It argues that the reason is the United States faces "three main sets of challengers—the revisionist powers of China and Russia, the rogue states of Iran and North Korea, and transnational threat organizations, particularly jihadist terrorist groups."

It points out in particular that "China and Russia challenge American power, influence, and interests, attempting to erode American security and prosperity. They are determined to make economies less free and less fair," etc. In such a circumstance, China has to do more in order to overcome the Kindleberger Trap. At the same time, China is supposed to do less in order to reduce the danger of the Thucydides Trap. China has to strike a balance between the needs of doing more and the pressure of doing less in providing international public goods. That is the dilemma faced by China when it simultaneously faces the Kindleberger Trap and the Thucydides Trap.

In addition to the challenges resulting from the above-mentioned two traps, China also faces a third trap, the Cold War Trap, in current international circumstances. The Cold War Trap is concerned with both the Thucydides Trap and the potential conflicts in terms of the ideological difference between China and the West. As correctly pointed out by Joseph S. Nye, with respect to the so-called Thucydides Trap between China and the United States, "there is nothing inevitable" because the effects of the trap are often exaggerated. In other words, it is possible for the two powers to avoid open conflicts if only because both sides know very clearly that costs of such conflicts are too high to afford.

However, in spite of this kind of possible positive prospect in evading open military conflicts, China and the United States will still face the danger of being involved in a cold war trap if both sides fail to address two sets of issues: One is to raise mutual strategic confidence, the other is to curb mutual contradictions in the ideological field. Past and current experiences suggest that neither of them is easy to substantiate. For both political and strategic reasons, mutual trust and mutual confidence are always something insufficient in Sino-U.S. relations in the past decades. With regard to the ideological factor, the negative reactions of the United States and some major European countries to China after the 19th National Congress of the CPC cast a strong shadow in this respect.

The texts of the National Security Strategy of the United States of America reveal the situation. Although it claims that "It is a strategy of principled realism that is guided by outcomes, not ideology," this claim is nevertheless misleading if one thinks that the America First National Security Strategy of the United States places values and ideology on the back burner. On the contrary, this document clearly lists the ideological factor as one of the four vital national interests that the United States "must protect in this competitive world."

The Trump Administration makes a systematic and quite coherent explanation about this stand by saying that "we will advance American influence because a world that supports American interests and reflects our values makes America more secure and prosperous. We will compete and lead in multilateral organizations so that American interests and principles are protected. America's commitment to liberty, democracy, and the rule of law serves as an inspiration for those living under tyranny." Based on this analysis, this document takes a rather harsh attitude towards China when talking about bilateral discrepancies not only in the economic and security fields, but also in the ideological realm.

For instance, the document asserts that "China and Russia want to shape a world antithetical to U.S. values and interests," and that "these are fundamentally political contests between those who favor repressive systems and those who favor free societies." European countries such as Germany and France also made some negative comments on China over the international order, approaches to global governance, and other issues.

The negative attitudes of Western countries in general, and of the United States in particular, suggest that pessimistic trends are on the rise in relations between China and major Western powers. This situation is of course not good for promoting peace, stability, and prosperity in the world. Therefore, concerned parties should make joint efforts to prevent these trends from further development, although it is not easy to stop, let alone reverse the trends. At least for China, this situation is obviously disappointing and more or less out of expectation. The gap between China's expectations and the response of the West suggests that something must have gone wrong with mutual perceptions between China and the West. It also implies that none of those negative trends is inevitable. To prevent the situation from further deteriorating, there should be efforts to strengthen mutual understanding and minimize misperceptions on both sides.

U.S. STATE SENATOR RICHARD BLACK

On the True Interest of the United States

Senator Richard Black is a member of the Virginia State Legislature. He made his presentation via pre-recorded video.

I'm Senator Dick Black and I'm pleased to join you for this important conference. My remarks will focus on the Mideast conflict and America's undeclared war against the Syrian people.

Our current actions against Syria are unlawful and they run counter to our vital national interest. More importantly, they represent a direct pathway to a much larger and far more dangerous and unpredictable war against Iran and its neighbors.

Syria is the center of gravity in the war on terror. In other words, its survival as a viable, intact state may very well determine the outcome of the global war on terror. Should American succeed in our long-held objective of toppling the legitimately elected Syrian government, this would lead to an unprecedented expansion of jihadist terror. Within months, Lebanon and

State Senator Richard Black

Jordan would fall, and this would likely embolden President Erdogan, the Turkish dictator, to drive hordes of battled-hardened jihadists from the battlefield to overrun the nations of Europe.

Some Personal History

For this reason, America's dogged opposition to the Syrian nation-state poses a clear and present danger to Europe and to all of civilization. Let me be clear: I'm not speaking as a pacifist. I served in uniform for 32 years. I was wounded fighting as a Forward Air Controller in the 1st Marine Regiment, and I made 70 combat patrols, generally at night, deep behind enemy lines. I was wounded during an attack, and both of my radiomen died fighting beside me. Before that, I flew 269 combat missions as a helicopter pilot. My aircraft was hit by enemy ground fire on four missions. Eventually, I served as a division chief in the office of the Judge Advocate General (JAG) at the Pentagon. There I prepared executive orders for the President's signature, and testified before Congress on behalf of the U.S. Army.

I say this to let you know that I love my country, I've bled for it. And I respect the men and women who obey the orders that they are given, when we send them over to war, even though I often think those orders are extraordinarily ill-advised.

I'm deeply concerned by the direction of American foreign policy, particularly as it affects Syria, because that nation is a vital gateway to Turkey, and thus, on to Europe itself.

Before the Syrian War

Before the Syrian War began in 2011, Syria was one of the five safest nations on Earth. It had the greatest women's rights and the greatest religious freedom of any of the Arab nations. It was debt free; it produced its own energy, food, many of its own manufactured products; its economy was very well balanced and it was self-sufficient. Syria had been at peace with Israel for 40 years. In 2013, just to demonstrate the secular nature of the government, Syria erected one of the world's greatest statues of Jesus Christ, and it towers over Israel, Lebanon, and Syria. Syria is a diverse and secular country. It is home to about 2 million Christians and 2 million Alawites. Now, the Alawites are a very highly modernized population. Additionally, Syria is home to Druze and large Sunni and smaller Shi'a populations of Muslims. The great majority of each religious group has supported the central government. The Grand Mufti Ahmad Hassoun is the spiritual leader of Syria's Sunni Muslims. Ahmad is an unwavering supporter of Syria's President Bashar al-Assad.

During the seven brutal years of the war, the Syrian nation of about 23 million has united, and withstood the combined forces of *two-thirds* of the world's military and industrial might; but despite this massive international pressure, there has not been a single assassination attempt against President Assad, who enjoys overwhelming and passionate support of the army and the people. Syria has faced the combined might of Americans, British, French, Israelis, Turks, Qataris, and Saudi Arabians.

Xinhua

Syrians celebrate the liberation of eastern Aleppo city in northern Syria, Dec. 22, 2016, with flags carrying the portrait of President Assad.

The United States Is at War with Syria

By any reasonable definition, the United States is at war with Syria. Since 2012, the United States has operated terrorist training camps in Jordan, Turkey, Qatar, Saudi Arabia, and now inside Syria, itself. We have supplied terrorists fighting Assad with tens of billions of dollars' worth of arms, ammunition, training, and payroll. This was done under the CIA's classified program, "Timber Sycamore." Once that program was disclosed, it was quickly terminated, but American-financed weapons, training, and manpower still flow freely to terrorists under other covert programs.

Despite this lengthy war of aggression, *not a single terrorist has ever become a popular figure* among the Syrian people, who remain doggedly loyal to President Assad and the Syrian armed forces. Recall that it was al-Qaeda that hijacked civilian airliners and flew them into the Twin Towers and the Pentagon on September 11, 2001, killing 3,000 Americans. Nonetheless, throughout the Syrian War, the United States has aligned with al-Qaeda and its affiliate against Syria. Virtually every so-called "moderate rebel group" has at one time or another fought shoulder to shoulder with al-Qaeda or ISIS. The dominant jihadists are sworn to behead all Christian and Alawite men and to make sex slaves of their wives, their daughters, and their children. For this reason, the success of the American venture in Syria could very well trigger one of the greatest genocides in recent history.

Contrary to Western propaganda, the war was never a popular uprising. President Assad did *not* take harsh measures against early demonstrators. In fact, he issued orders requiring riot control troops to carry wooden batons instead of rifles. As a consequence, many died at the hands of al-Qaeda and the Muslim Brotherhood before he finally relented and permitted them to protect themselves with loaded weapons.

Chemical Weapons Attacks are Fake News

Let me address the often-cited claim that Assad has used poison gas, crossing some "red line." That claim is patently false: The same propaganda ploy was used first by the CIA, as a pretext to launch the invasion of Iraq. That deceit proved so successful in laying the groundwork for the Iraq War, that it has been used several times during the conflict in Syria to blame President Assad for "gassing his own people." This lie has duped Americans into being drawn ever deeper into the Syrian War. But ask yourself this question: "If Syria wanted to use poison gas, why would they use it on toddlers and their parents, instead of using it to defend against ISIS and al-Qaeda in the desperate battles raging across the country?"

Now, poison gas is not used in pinprick attacks against civilian targets. If it is used, it is employed massively, in conjunction with large-scale, offensive maneuvers on the battlefield. Each of the three false-flag attacks, staged by al-Qaeda and its allies, was convincingly disproved by the world's most respected investigative journalist, Pulitzer Prize winning reporter Seymour Hersh—the man who wrote the story of the My Lai Massacre in Vietnam, and the Abu Ghraib prison misconduct in Iraq. He has greater access to the inner workings of the CIA and Pentagon than any other journalist today. It would be totally irrational for President Assad to employ poison gas given the predictable backlash and the total absence of *any* military benefit to Syria.

The Spoils of Perpetual Wars

The United States has long planned regime change in Syria. According to Gen. Wesley Clark, the former Supreme Allied Commander in Europe, America first began drafting war plans to topple Syria in 2001. WikiLeaks published actual secret plans that were developed by the U.S. Embassy in Damascus in 2006. Those plans laid out detailed steps to destabilize and topple the legitimate government of Syria. In 2010, Hillary Clinton became Secretary of State. She executed plans to overthrow Libya to capture its arsenal of

Courtesy of Sen. Black

President Bashar al Assad (left) meets Virginia State Sen. Richard Black in Damascus, April 28, 2016.

weapons and use them to arm terrorists in Syria. When Libya's leader, Col. Muammar Qaddafi, was murdered in 2011, we invaded Libya under the guise of a "no-fly zone." We quickly gave the Turks control of a Libyan air field and then began flying plundered Libyan weapons into Turkey using Qatari aircraft. The first aircraft that was sent from Libya also carried 700 Tunisian terrorists, who were then sent across the Turkish border, and into Syria.

From 2011 until today, the United States has fought to topple the popularly elected government of Bashar al-Assad and install a puppet regime. But why are we fighting in Syria at all? In fact, what are we fighting for *anywhere* in the Middle East? Our own actions have spawned huge armies of ISIS and al-Qaeda terrorists. Without us there, both Iraq and Syria would soon eliminate the last vestiges of these terror groups and restore order to their own nations. So, are we fighting to serve U.S.—or foreign—interests? And, are we simply deploying courageous American troops as a sort of Foreign Legion for hire?

Crown Prince Mohammed bin Salman, the brutal dictator of Saudi Arabia, was overheard saying, "I have Kushner in my pocket." Some believe that Jared Kushner, who had access to Presidential intelligence, may have revealed the names of Saudis who were disloyal to the Crown Prince shortly before the Saudi dictator launched his brutal crackdown on those same dissidents. Is this all being done for personal gain?

Now certainly war profiteers have amassed enormous fortunes through these wars. And we know that our coalition partners, Qatar, Saudi Arabia, want to topple the Syrian government and run lucrative oil and gas pipelines across Syria's sovereign territory.

But, you know, I am amazed at Americans' acquiescence in perpetual Mideast war. No one even mentions an end to hostilities and a return to peace. By contrast, it's instructive to recall that we only fought in World War I for 17 months, before politicians were forced to promise that that would be the "war to end all wars."

Now think of this: After 17 years, we remain committed to several simultaneous wars with no end in sight. It's breaking our military forces down and it is bankrupting the nation. How many Americans realize that *fully one-third of the entire U.S. national debt* has been incurred through our Middle Eastern wars? Despite American lives lost, soldiers maimed, and treasure wasted; despite one and one-half million Libyans, Afghans, Yemenis, Iraqis, and Syrians killed; despite trillions in property destruction—I cannot point to a *single thing* that these wars have done for the American people, or for the vital national interests of the United States. Instead, we've generated massive strings of refugees, who are hostile to Western values and determined to undermine European cultures.

We started these wars facing a small contingent of terrorists. Well, here we are a generation later: We've multiplied their ranks a thousand-fold, by arming, training, and financing these same terrorists. We've given them real-world battlefield experience, making them the most combat-ready forces on Earth today.

This, in my view, is suicidal madness. The enormous fear and resentment we have generated have obliterated generations of good will. This makes it a near certainty that China will soon displace, through peaceful means, the trade and influence the United States has tried to exact through fear and terror. Unless we develop a strategy for peace, China will displace us as the world's dominant power. Our present strategy amounts to regime change by raining down bombs, collapsing homes, and blowing bodies into the streets. By contrast, China quietly builds highways, factories, dams, infrastructure, without instigating violent coups. Now which approach will appeal to foreign nations? Given the choice, they will inevitably opt for China's roads, bridges, dams, and factories over the American bombs, destruction, and bloodshed.

Just take a look at Iraq: From 1990, when the Gulf War first began, until today, the United States bombed that country almost incessantly. During the 28-year bombing campaign, we've dropped over a third of a million bombs on Iraq and the number is still rising. Just this past week, we, or our ally Israel, bombed Iraq's Popular Mobilization Forces (PMF), killing 22 and wounding 12. At that time, those Iraqis were fighting ISIS, our supposed enemy. So this week's attack rounds out the 28th year of hostile actions on Iraqi territory, against a nation that, just like Syria, has *never* once taken hostile action against the United States.

Now, returning to Syria: The United States, which once promised "no boots on the ground," is likely to have as many as 8,000 soldiers, marines, and contractors, stationed in Syria today. We built at least 11 bases in northeast Syria, a fact that Turkey disclosed in 2017 to our enormous consternation. U.S. troops are presently embarked on a mission to carve out a tenuous landlocked state, by granting the Kurdish minority dominance over predominantly Arab lands in northeast Syria. This region, lying between the Euphrates River and the Turkish border, comprises about 30% of Syria's land mass.

While Syria is sparsely populated, it holds much of the oil, gas, and agricultural wealth that sustains the entire Syrian people. Should this American "Plan B" succeed in splitting Syria apart, the nation's people will be permanently impoverished—all so the United States can block ancient trade routes linking Syria, Iraq, and Iran. This appears to be part of a strategy to pave the groundwork for a far greater war yet to come.

But There is Great Hope in and for Syria

But there is great hope in Syria. The Syrian armed forces and its allies have liberated 90% of Syria's population. Since Russia intervened in 2015, Syria has scored an unbroken string of battlefield victories. Almost all of its major cities have been liberated by the Syrian Army. It's only the resistance of the United States, Israel, and Turkey, that prevents a rapid conclusion to the war. It's high time for the United States to depart from Syria, and to leave the Middle East. If we leave, there will be a time of peace and reconciliation. Refugees will return, and rebuilding will accelerate.

Since its liberation by Syrian forces in 2016, almost one-half million Syrians have returned to the Syria's second largest city, Aleppo. The United States could make an impressive humanitarian gesture, simply by lifting its naval blockade of Syria, and by releasing the monetary restrictions, in order to end the starvation, the poverty, the deprivation of medical supplies that we've inflicted on their people.

Americans are a good and decent people. Our nation is better than our foreign policy would suggest. We need to stop inflicting violence by supporting terrorist groups and restore peace to the world.

Thank you very much.

LT. COL. ULRICH SCHOLZ

Interest Monsters: Democracy, Human Rights and Other Hypocrisies

Lt. Col. (ret.) Ulrich Scholz is a former NATO planner. This is an edited report, combining his prepared address with the transcript of his speech. He spoke on Panel I, June 30, 2018.

Good morning. Thank you very much, Mrs. LaRouche and Mr. LaRouche, for having me here again to speak what's on my mind and in my heart. I was here two years ago, and talked about war as a pathology of the West. Just a few words about myself. I flew, in the first third of my military career, Phantoms and Tornadoes. In the second third, I planned wars. In my third, in my military education, I understood war. And now, I'm in my final stage of learning, and I am trying to find out why we still engage in wars, and how we can change that.

I'd like to start with George Bernard Shaw, who once said, "Sometimes I like to quote myself. It puts spice in the conversation." I'll quote myself here: In March 2003, I was at Queen's University at Kingston, teaching on the subject of security policy, and I gave a speech to local business and political people. Six weeks prior to that speech, President George W. Bush had invaded Iraq, and that was my topic. My American colleague on the left argued for the war, and I argued against the war. And sometimes, I didn't know what was going to happen; but my feeling was that if we didn't put the UN in charge of the world, we would end up where we are now. And we ended up there.

After that, I went through several educational processes. I thought about how to change the UN—I now think it's not an organizational change we need. I think the problem is not the structure of the organization—the problem is that the UN, which failed in its main mission of keeping peace in the world, needs instead to concentrate more on brokering interests. This word interests—

Lt. Col. (ret.) Ulrich Scholz

I've heard it many times this morning—is very important. I think the problem is that nations have interests, and we don't pay attention to those, especially the big ones. The second is the human element when we talk about interests. We are humans and what works on the micro-level, with families and individuals, has a record of working very well when applied seriously. When we try to resolve political conflict, we disregard this aspect. We often view NATO and the U.S. government organizations, but forget that inside those organizations there are human beings. We should focus more on how we get those people in those organizations together.

Let us not forget the hypocrisies in international relations. The West has waged war since 1990, many times—Kosovo, Libya, Iraq several times, and Afghanistan. All these wars were always begun with an alibi: "We do it on behalf of the international community"—whatever that is. Or the UN flag is used under the banner, "responsibility to protect," or "humanitarian intervention." I argue, and I can prove it—I won't go into that full proof today—that these are all alibis. These are hypocrisies. The real reason the West goes to war is for interests.

The following is from the prepared address.

The World Needs an Effective UN

Since its founding in 1945, the main mission of the UN as a world organization has been to keep the peace. Despite all merit due in creating a kind of international order, the many wars and conflicts that have taken place since then are sad proof that the organization has failed in its main mission.

I would like to suggest that we understand and use the UN more as a global interest moderator rather than a peacekeeper. Because, by focusing on the first, success in the second is much more likely; and last but not least, the UN as an effective broker of interests could become the driver for projects like the New Silk Road.

In my short presentation I am going to make the argument that the main reasons for the UN's failure to keep the peace, and for the resistance to the New Silk Road Project from some international figures, are the disregard for the importance of interests of all international actors and the neglect of the human dimension in dealing with those interests. Since the end of the Cold War in 1990, democratic states have waged war and violated their ethics quite a few times. They waged war in the Balkans, in Iraq, in Afghanistan, in Libya, and in Syria. In doing so they also killed those whom they pretended to protect. They invented ethical terms like "responsibility to protect" and "humanitarian intervention" to cover up their real intention for going to war: National Interests!

At the beginning of the air campaign to liberate Kuwait from Iraqi occupation, U.S. Air Force General Chuck Horner, commander of allied air forces of Desert Shield/Desert Storm, told his pilots to break off an attack and bring back their bombs if they ran the risk of being shot down. He said that there was no target in the whole of Iraq worth dying for. I would like to alter his statement to make it a universal one: There is no target in the world worth killing for.

The Philosophical Foundation

America's post-World War II foreign policy has been greatly influenced by Hans Joachim Morgenthau, a German-born American political scientist whose basic idea of an all-mighty state refers back to Thomas Hobbes' *The Leviathan*. In 1948, Morgenthau published his work on foreign policy, *Politics among Nations*. It contains the essential ideas of "Political Realism."

The following four ideas are my selection. They reflect the history of states from 1648 (the Peace of Westphalia) until today. The first idea is almost a no-brainer:

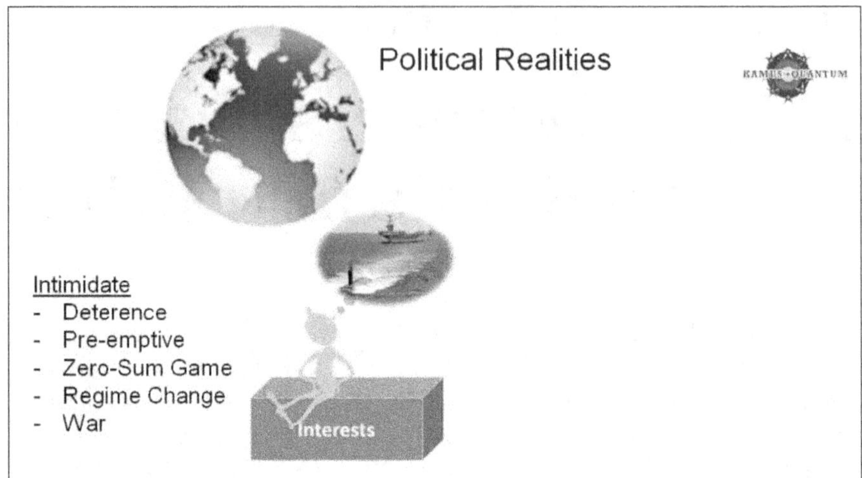

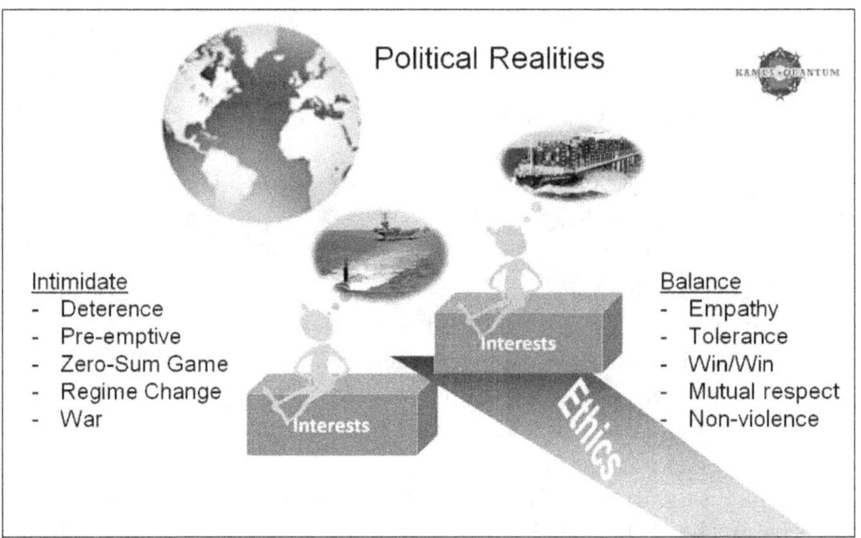

Political power serves interests. Countries and peoples have interests, and it is the duty of their leaders to use their power to secure them. The next three ideas, I call essentials: Balancing not intimidating, Values are interests = hypocrisy, and thirdly, Limits of universal values. I call these essentials because they contain the main reasons why politicians fail to secure the interests of their peoples.

Morgenthau's arguments against the Vietnam War support this argument. I dare to say that all wars America and the West have waged since Vietnam have not been in the interest of their peoples for the same reasons.

Balancing Interests vs. Intimidation

To make my argument, I would like to focus on Essential Number Two. It is here that post-Cold-War neo-

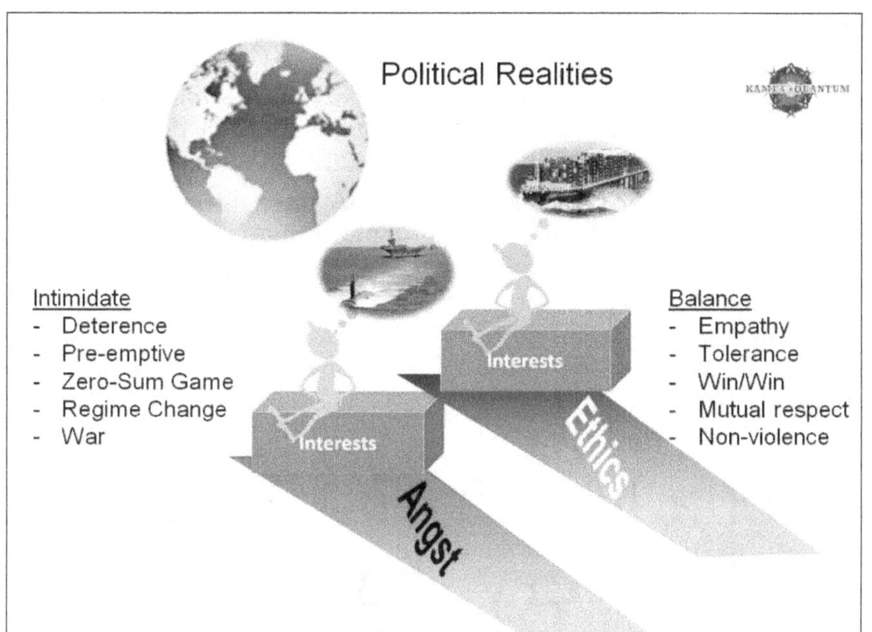

worse, such as global terrorism or nuclear war. Lasting security, based on one's own interests, is achieved best if those interests are balanced in a mutually benefitting way.

At this point I would like to come in with ethics, which are not an Interest per se. The real power lies in living ethically, not in preaching ethics. A foreign policy based on balancing interests rests on human values: empathy, tolerance, and mutual respect.

Ethics flows like an underground river. If we allow intimidation to run foreign policy, the underground river carrying intimidation is called Angst.

Trust and Education

When people of different countries, political systems, and cultures meet to resolve conflicts and to balance interests, it is important that they know, understand, and like each other. The ultimate goal is trust, which should not just be the result of empathy, but sympathy. Relations developed in such a way must be set up on a long term basis (years!). The people selected should be of special character with outstanding soft skills in an intercultural realm. They don't have to be the subject matter experts, rather they should be facilitators at the

conservative politicians in the United States deviate from classical realism. Instead of trying to balance interests with other stakeholders in the realm of foreign policy, they either go to war as they did in Iraq, Afghanistan, Libya, and Syria, or they intimidate others as they are (have been) doing with Russia, North Korea, and Iran. I argue that in all these conflicts they have failed to secure American interests.

But intimidation not only jeopardizes one's own interests. It also increases the risk of armed conflict, which entails the danger of escalating to something

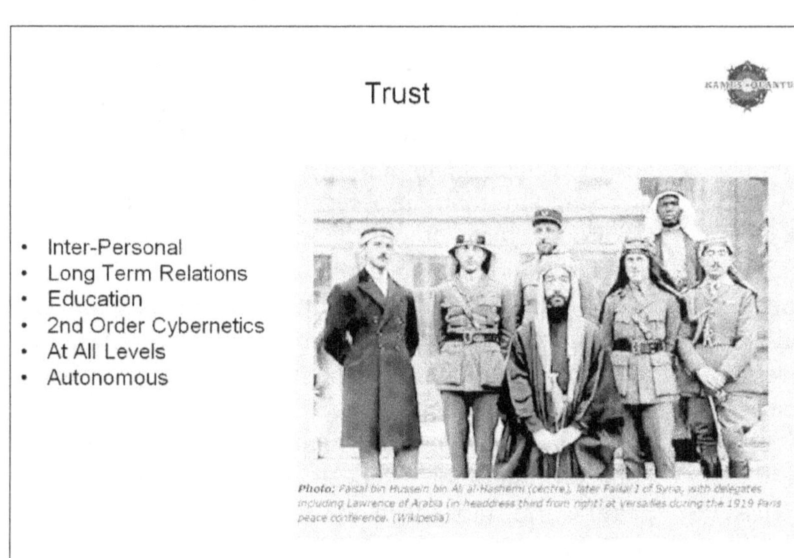

Photo: Faisal bin Hussein bin Ali al-Hashemi (centre), later Faisal I of Syria, with delegates including Lawrence of Arabia (in headdress third from right) at Versailles during the 1919 Paris peace conference. [Wikipedia]

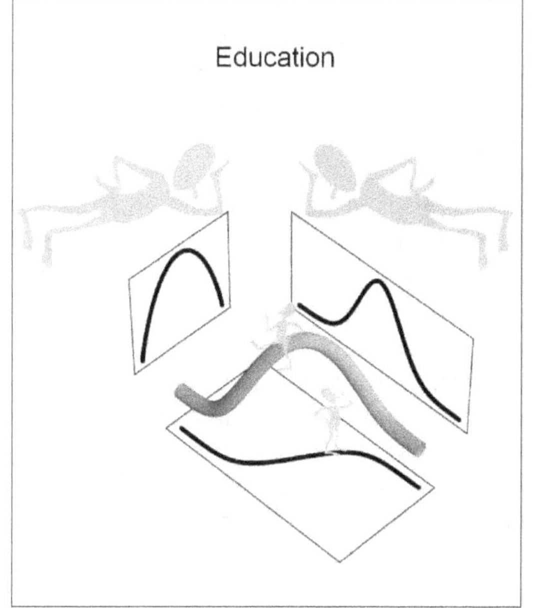

various levels of cooperation, governmental and non-governmental. Outside the functionalities of projects, their interaction should be autonomous. Cooperation should be driven mainly by the spirit of the common goal and not so much by organizational interests of the day.

One final word on education. I consider failed communications as one of the main reasons for violent conflict resolutions, which is not a matter of language but a matter of perceiving and thinking. Conflict parties discuss their differences in the first order of cybernetics, not understanding that they are dealing with second order problems. I suggest therefore that everybody who is in the business of conflict resolution and balancing interests should get a thorough education in systems theory and the philosophy behind it. There cannot be any objectivity, because "Everything that is said, is said by an observer."

COLONEL (RET.) ALAIN CORVEZ

The U.S. Refusal of a Multipolar World Makes the Transition Very Painful

Col. Alain Corvez is an international consultant and former Counsellor for the French Defense and Interior Ministries. This is a summary report of his speech, which was presented in French on Panel 1, June 30, 2018.

Speaking in French, Col. Corvez said at the start that he felt much inspired by all the previous speakers, that particularly Senator Black's remarks reflected an "extreme reality" which poses the main problem. Trump is challenged by the Deep State in the United States, the covert oligarchy which forced him to continue the military interventions, this being a brutal policy which is not in the interest of the real Europe—which de Gaulle called the "Europe of the Nations." The European Union of today is a technocratic, supranational regime. For France, the question is when will France finally denounce Saudi Arabia and Qatar for their aggressive policies in the Mideast, against Syria and Yemen? The sanctions against Iran which the EU decreed are also not in the real European interest, because the Europeans have to cooperate with Iran and with Russia. The sanctions have not had the planned effect on Iran

Col. (ret.) Alain Corvez

because the Iranian nation supports its government.

On the North Korean problem, the Singapore Summit between Trump and Kim Jong-un is opening the door to demilitarization and denuclearization of the Korean Peninsula, which is a break from the last years of aggressive and brutal policy against other nations by the United States. This shows that neither confrontation nor war solve problems: solution can only come from dialogue. A rapprochement is under way, with South Korea moving closer to cooperation with Russia and China. India and Japan are also reviewing their policies in the region. Although there are still many problems, the world is on its way toward a future without the nuclear Damocles' Sword that is still threatening all of humanity today. The recent SCO summit presented a healthy alternative to the G-7 Summit of the Old Paradigm powers. That summit represented 42% of the world population, opting for peace, cooperation and development. De Gaulle once said in a 1964 speech to Mexican students, that if the threat of nuclear obliteration can be averted, the road is free to a better world, and indeed, the offer is there today to build such a world.

The President Trump Europeans Do Not Know

Roger Stone is a U.S. political strategist of the Trump faction in the Republican Party. He made his presentation by live video.

First of all, I want to apologize for the fact that I cannot join you personally. I very much appreciate and [inaudible] and the Schiller Institute, and my good friend Harley Schlanger, who arranged for this video presentation.

I also want to salute the Schiller Institute and Helga Zepp-LaRouche for your forward-thinking agenda and your commitment to economic and financial reform, which I believe, with the assistance of the Trump Administration, can remake our global thinking entirely and move us towards more peace and prosperity on a worldwide basis.

I am very familiar with the extraordinary and prophetic thinking of Lyndon LaRouche, having encountered him in New Hampshire in 1980, during the Republican primary for President of the United States. And, as a former aide to President Ronald Reagan, I recognize the important backstage role that Lyndon LaRouche played in the last election of a non-neo-con outsider, as President of the United States.

I must say, that in 1980, I was more of a conventional conservative Republican, and at that time, I thought Dr. LaRouche's views were somewhat exotic. Today, I would say, however, that I have evolved to recognize the role of an evil, two-party duopoly, that has, unfortunately, run the United States into a ditch.

The two-party duopoly of the Bushes and the Clintons, working together, has given us endless foreign wars, where our apparent national interests were never apparent; erosion of our civil liberties, with a government that keeps meta-data tags on Americans, reads our emails, monitors our text messages, catalogues our phone calls; gave us trade policies which were based on

Schiller Institute

Roger Stone

"one size fits all" international trade agreements, which appeared to be beneficial to our trading partners, but on rare occasion equally beneficial to the United States. We have pursued immigration policies that cheated those who were waiting on line to get into the country and obtain their citizenship legally, to the benefit of those who jumped the line and entered the country illegally, and in many cases, left our streets and neighborhoods unsafe.

I am a 40-year friend and associate of Donald Trump, and the evolution in my thinking opinion between 1980 and 1988, led me to believe that Trump was the one man with the stature, the courage, and the independence from the failed policies of the two-party duopoly that has run our country, and that he should seek the Presidency. I sought to convince him to become a candidate as early as 1988. I sought again to convince him to become a candidate in 2000, and again in 2012. And then, finally, successfully, in 2016.

Now, I would concede to you, that despite my early enthusiasm, the time was probably not yet ripe for a Trump-style candidacy. It is the first time Americans have gone outside a career politician or a military hero, in order to select a business person as a President. Unthinkable, as early as 1980, perhaps. Perhaps, it was unthinkable in 2000. But after a [inaudible] eight years of the Obama Presidency, the stage was set for a reform-oriented President who was committed to stronger and better relations with both Russia and China, and who rejected the new world order as put forward by President George H.W. Bush and furthered by his son, President George W. Bush—an agenda that was seamlessly pursued, whether the President was Republican or Democrat, whether our President was a Clinton or a Bush.

We now have a scandal in the United States, in

which claims of Russian "collusion" are used to mask what is, in fact, the greatest political scandal in our history: And that is, the use of the power and the authority of the state to spy on and undermine the candidacy of the Republican nominee for President. In fact, having been a veteran of the Nixon Administration, I recognize that Nixon was removed from power because men who were associated with his campaign, were caught breaking into the Watergate facility, to plant bugs (which never really worked) to spy on his opponent and the Democrats. He was also removed, because men who were associated with his campaign were caught infiltrating the campaigns of his opponents, Sen. Hubert Humphrey, and then, later, Sen. George McGovern.

FBI

Former FBI Director Robert Mueller (right) is recognized by President Obama at a ceremony announcing the nomination of James Comey (left) as FBI Director. White House Rose Garden, June 21, 2013.

Anti-Trump Scandal Worse than Watergate

The scandal which we are looking at today, is far more egregious! At least in the case of Nixon, and it was never proved that Nixon himself approved *any* of these illegal activities,— but in the case of Nixon, the individuals who were apprehended were private citizens. Here we have a far more egregious abuse of power: It is the use of the state's authority and its extraordinary technological capability, to hijack the 2016 election and subvert democracy itself, in an attempt to wire the election for Hillary Clinton.

The entire Russiagate investigation, the totally unproven charges of Russian collusion, are a smokescreen, to mask those illegal activities by the Obama Administration in its attempt to hijack our last election, referred to in the text messages of FBI agent Peter Strzok as "the insurance policy." We now know that the FBI, under Barack Obama, infiltrated the Trump campaign as early as May of 2016—far earlier than it admits opening its investigations into alleged "Russian collusion" by the Trump campaign.

The role of British intelligence in all of this, cannot be underestimated. We know that Prof. Stefan Halper was approaching members of the Trump campaign—at the lowest possible level, I might mention—in an attempt to plant evidence of Russian collusion. It is almost laughable that the *Washington Post* and the *New York Times* continue to claim that the activities of Halper, the activities of others, were an attempt to ferret out Russian collusion, when in fact, they were attempts to plant *faux* Russian collusion to be discovered later, in an effort to undermine Trump in the seemingly unlikely event of Trump's victory.

I never had any doubts about Trump's ability to win the 2016 election. It's important to recognize that 2016 was the year in which the mainstream media lost their monopoly stranglehold on political discourse. This is due only to the rise of a vibrant and robust alternative media, which in turn, has given far greater currency to the ideas and principles of Lyndon LaRouche, to the ideas and principles of Donald Trump, to reset the world stage for cooperative trading partnerships and relationships with both the Russians and the Chinese, and put an end to the neo-con policies of war and bankruptcy, which the mainstream media have continued to pursue, quite sadly, with vigor.

Sadly, what we see today in the United States, and perhaps across the world, is an attempt to put the toothpaste back in the tube. That is to say, a war of Internet censorship which seeks to silence voices such as mine, and my friends at Infowars, for example, alternative media outlets like *Breitbart* and the *Daily Caller* and others who espouse Trumpism, and remove them—from Facebook, from Twitter, from YouTube—it's a war of eradication, and an attempt to strangle our First Amendment rights under the U.S. Constitution, and to use monopolistic practices and anti-competitive business practices to end our free speech and our access to this wonderful medium of the Internet which makes our dialogue, here, today, entirely possible.

I must say that the prospects for a Trump-Putin summit in July, have raised the hackles in some corners of Washington, D.C., as well as Whitehall, to a level of near-hysteria. President Donald Trump is one who believes that when your adversaries possess thermonuclear weapons, as well as vast economic power, that one is much better off in a dialogue with them, than in a Cold War. And therefore, I firmly believe that his trip to Helsinki to meet Vladimir Putin is a mission of peace, a mission of future economic cooperation, and perhaps of joint cooperation to eradicate those Islamic extremist elements that seek to damage both of our nations.

U.S. National Security Advisor John Bolton (right) meets with Russian President Vladimir Putin to prepare for Trump/Putin summit. The Kremlin, June 27, 2018.

Mueller Went after LaRouche, Now after Trump and Me

What is going on in the United States—the persecution of a number of President Trump's key advisors, is reminiscent of the kind of tactics that were used against Lyndon LaRouche by the Bushes in the 1980s. One of the principal reasons I am unable to join you in person, is that, as you may have read, Special Counsel Robert Mueller—unable to prove any "Russian collusion" on my part, unable to prove any collaboration with WikiLeaks with respect to its devastating disclosures regarding the Democratic National Committee and Hillary Clinton, unable to prove or provide any evidence that I had any knowledge of the release of John Podesta's emails in advance—now seeks to come up and conjure, perhaps fabricate and manufacture, some other charge against me, perhaps relating to my business, or my finances, or my tactics.

This is the same Robert Mueller who harassed Lyndon LaRouche in the 1980s, who now seeks to persecute me, simply because of my support for President Donald Trump.

I'm being sued by the Democratic National Committee; I'm being sued by an Obama-affiliated group called Project Democracy; I'm being sued by a Chinese billionaire—all of these sore-loser lawsuits are without merit, but exceedingly expensive. On top of which, now, I now must fend off the efforts of Robert Mueller to bring some bogus charges against me, in his attempt to either silence me, or to seek my cooperation in testifying against my friend of almost 40 years, Donald J. Trump. *This will not happen.*

My friends have set up a legal defense fund for me, at Stone Defense Fund.com. I must say that contributions from foreign nationals are perfectly permissible and those who wish to make a contribution will have my heartfelt thanks. I face an extraordinarily difficult and defensive battle as the Deep State has targetted me, because of my long association with Donald Trump, and my commitment to his non-interventionist foreign policy and his policy of economic revitalization of the United States.

Trump Bashed for Successes at Home and Abroad

We have seen a precipitous rise in violence in the United States, and a near-hysteria on the left, which is based almost solely on the increasing success and popularity of the Trump policies. We will have in excess of 4% economic growth in the next quarter. We were told under President Barack Obama that this rate of GDP growth was structurally impossible. They were wrong.

We have seen the creation of 1 million new jobs, 228,000 in the month of May alone. We have seen the President on the cusp of a historic peace deal in the Koreas, and perhaps the successful denuclearization of a nation long-considered our greatest foe. How ironic, that the President has pursued a peace deal in the Koreas, that if it had been achieved by Barack Obama would be called "brilliant" by the mainstream media; but because it is achieved by Donald Trump, they call it "risky."

The President pursues non-interventionist, peace-oriented policies and a reform agenda in terms of revitalizing our economy, in terms of reforming our immigration system, in terms of redoing our trade agreements, so that they are of reciprocal value; and in terms of reaching new relationships with both the Russians and the Chinese, built on our joint desire for peace and prosperity.

I have every confidence in this President. But I do not underestimate the Deep State's efforts to destroy his Presidency and to remove him. It was reported by *Bloomberg News*, only yesterday, that Robert Mueller, the same hit man for the Bushes who targeted Lyndon LaRouche decades ago, will decide about raising charges against the President in his final report, this fall. How convenient! Just before the 2018 midterm elections.

The previous day, *Bloomberg News* reported that now, Robert Mueller would focus on the issue of "Russian collusion." That's extraordinary. He's been at it for two years, and has spent in excess of $17 million of our taxpayers' money. I thought that he *was* focused on "Russian collusion." As the attempts to harass me demonstrate, his investigation has nothing to do with "Russian collusion." As Mr. Mueller seeks any process-related crime, pertaining to the termination of FBI Director James Comey, an extraordinarily corrupt public figure, or to the dismissal of Gen. Mike Flynn, a true American patriot, who was also subject to harassment and legal undermining by Robert Mueller and his cabal of thugs.

So, the prospects for the Trump Presidency are strong, because as his political strength grows, as his public support in the country is galvanized, it gives him a freer hand to deal with the Mueller outrage, and to deal with the fact that he has a partisan prosecutor who has been given broad and unfettered legal power by Trump's own Justice Department, and quislings such as Deputy Attorney General Rod Rosenstein, who seek nothing less than to undo what they could not do at the ballot box in 2016.

President Donald Trump with Chairman Kim Jong-un of the Democatic People's Republic of Korea in Singapore, June 12, 2018.

A Field Manual for Victory

I'm delighted to have the opportunity to join you! As some of you may know, my sixth book, *Stone's Rules*, is now widely available. I would put this book up there with Machiavelli's *The Prince*, or Sun Tzu's *The Art of War*, as a field manual for victory, that is applicable for any person, regardless of their chosen avocation. Whether you are in business, or politics, or technology, or media, or fashion, or even agriculture, these are the tested rules of the road, the hard lessons that I have learned in 40 years in the American arena. I commend this book to you, you can buy it through Amazon or Barnes & Noble. I think most reputable book purveyors in the country have it available, and I think you will enjoy it.

I thank you very much for your kind invitation to address you today. I look forward to a new world, based on the leadership of an American President who is deeply committed to a new set of policies, rejecting the policies of the neo-cons and their British co-conspirators, and fostering a new spirit of world peace and cooperation. I have urged the President to study the Silk Road policies that you are so enthusiastic about, and which I have come to embrace.

I salute you, and I thank you so much for your time this morning. Thank you.

How the Belt and Road Initiative Is Changing Africa: The Only Human Solution to the Refugee Crisis

HUSSEIN ASKARY

Opening Remarks

Hussein Askary, Southwest Asia Coordinator for the Schiller Institute, introduced Panel II of the Schiller Institute conference on June 20.

Thank you very much, Claudio. I'm pleased and honored to be opening this esteemed and very interesting panel.

My name is Hussein Askary; I am an Iraqi Swedish citizen. I'm the Southwest Asia Coordinator for the Schiller Institute. I've been working with the Schiller Institute for the last 23 years. I'm also the co-author of the Schiller Institute Special Report, *Extending the New Silk Road to West Asia and Africa*, which was released in November 2017 at a conference here, in this same place. This report, of which we have copies—everybody should get copies—is a wonderful expression of the optimism that has been sparked by Africa's joining the New Paradigm, defined by the Belt and Road Initiative of 2013

Hussein Askary

presented by China, and by the BRICS nations' Fortaleza Declaration of 2014.

Most African nations are working intensively now on real development plans with China and the other nations of the BRICS and their friends. This report is also a road map for the bright future that is awaiting the coming generations of Africans and the people of Southwest Asia, the so-called "Middle East." Middle East is the wrong term—it's called Southwest Asia.

Africa Is a Wonderful Continent

This is Africa by night. We have a true image of Africa by night, taken by NASA satellites, and you see a continent shrouded in darkness, because there is simply no electricity. The image of Africa in 2050 is an image drawn from my instructions, by our friend and member, Chance McGee, of how we envision Africa to

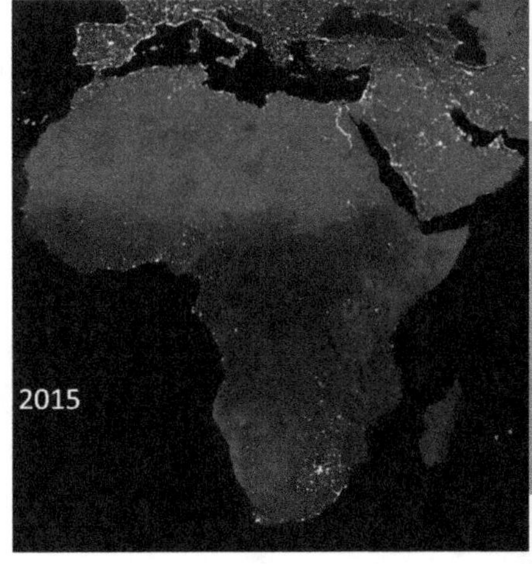

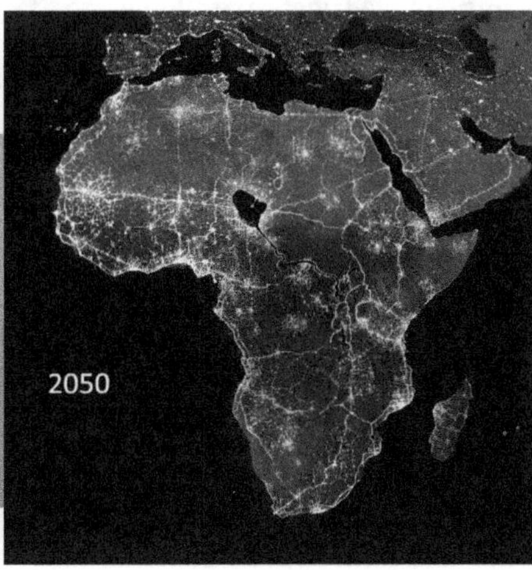

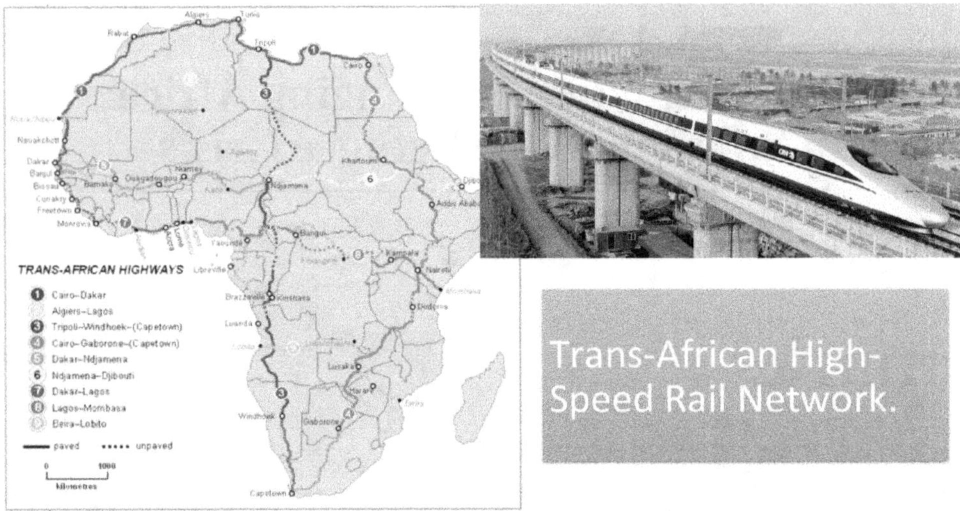

Trans-African High-Speed Rail Network.

this is the lesson we are learning from China's involvement in Africa.

I'm not going to describe this report in detail, because I did so last year, and people should just get a copy of the report. Some of the projects described in this report are already completed, some are under construction or being seriously negotiated. As some of our honorable speakers will testify, enormous progress is taking place. At least one nation in Africa, Ethiopia, is now nicknamed a "double-digit growth nation." And many others will soon join the club.

look by night in 2050.

By 2030, Southwest Asia and Africa will have jointly contributed the greatest population growth, of all world regions, reaching an estimated 1.9 billion by 2030, with an amazing median age of only 23 years. By 2050, the bulk of the world's population growth will take place in Africa. Of an additional 2.4 billion people projected to be born between 2015 and 2050, 1.3 billion will be added in Africa. While people who have been brainwashed by British propaganda believe this is a catastrophe, and a problem, we believe this is a fantastic challenge and a great opportunity.

And I think this is the same view that China holds of Africa. If we listen to speeches by President Xi Jinping in the China-Africa summits, he sees Africa as a great opportunity. What is required, as Helga Zepp-LaRouche said this morning, is that to get to the New Paradigm, for Europe to join the New Paradigm, it's not only that they will participate in building railways in Africa—we have to change our view of humans, and our attitudes, for example, towards Africa! Because Africa, in European minds and in the United States, is associated with problems, because that's the only thing being reported. So instead, we have to get a change in the mind of the European policymakers, and in the population in the United States, that Africa is not a problem: Africa is a great challenge, but it is a great opportunity. I think

There are no limits to what can be achieved on this wonderful continent, and therefore, our level of ambition and visions, and our plans, have to be at the same level as the challenge itself. This is a map of the trans-African high-speed railway we envision. This plan has existed in the African Union for many, many years, but it is represented as highways that have never been built. But now the rail is being developed piece by piece.

Like the Djibouti-Addis Ababa railway that was completed in 2017, with the help of China, we have the Mombasa-Nairobi railway, which was also completed last year. These projects are breaking all previous records—on construction, speed, efficiency, and cost. So these are some of the projects.

The plan that the African Union has been dreaming

Mombasa-Nairobi Railway and East African Master Plan

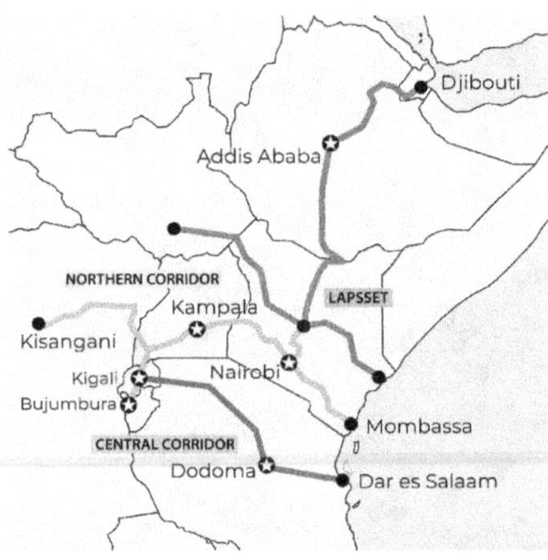

of and planning for, is now being implemented on the ground. The proverbial shovel is already in the ground. This is not something that is going to happen sometime in the future.

Our panel, titled "How the Belt and Road Initiative Is Changing Africa: The Only Human Solution to the Refugee Crisis," could not come together at a more crucial time than this. As the old paradigm unfortunately continues to wreak havoc in many nations, such as in Syria and Yemen, the consequences of at least forty years of misguided and intentionally destructive policies imposed on these nations are still being felt through widespread poverty, epidemics, food shortages, and lack of basic services, and also in the mass refugee crisis.

I Was a Refugee, Myself

I was myself a refugee, and suffered enormously with my family when we had to flee Iraq in 1991, from the Kurdish city of Sulaymaniyah in Iraq, as a consequence of the Gulf War—Desert Storm—which Colonel Scholz was talking about [see Panel 1], launched by George Bush, Sr. We had to walk, my family and I, for six days and nights, in the very harsh mountain climate; it was raining and even snowing in some cases. We had nothing with us, except small bags of dried fruit, until we reached the Iranian border, and then we ended up in huge tent camps in Iran.

When we reached these refugee camps, it was a terrible situation for morale. The physical conditions were terrible, but we managed to dust off our clothes and rise—my family and I, my sisters, especially—and we started working with the international aid organizations, the Red Cross and Doctors Without Borders. One year later, I managed to come to Norway. I was the featured person in a 1994 documentary film in Norway about the refugee crisis. It was a documentary series, called "Sightseeing in Reality: One of the Lucky Ones," referring to me. I was 23 years old at the time.

As Helga said today, you know, when you look at refugees, they're not objects on the TV screen. When you look at refugees, they are real human beings—many of them have aspirations, they have a mission in their lives, and they're not just a number.

Two years later, after I reached Norway in 1992, I

Refugees fleeing in 1991 during Operation Desert Storm from Sulaymaniyah, Iraq, through a very harsh mountain climate, to a camp in Iran.

met the Schiller Institute in Oslo. So I have a firsthand sense of what it means to suffer as a refugee, and to leave everything behind and risk your life to get to where you believe is a safer place, or where you can live with dignity.

However, I was convinced that the solution to all the many refugee crises was not by relieving the symptoms, by simply providing aid to the refugees—which should be done, anyway, you should help refugees—but by dealing with the causes of all these crises at the core. That could and will only be dealt with, through creating a new and just world economic order, and political order.

So, it was all very natural for me to join the Schiller Institute in 1994, and dedicate my time and energy to contribute to creating this new paradigm, with Helga and Lyndon LaRouche and all the wonderful people I have met and worked with all these years.

So, whether you are a refugee, a native, a citizen, a resident of Europe or the United States or anywhere, you should join the Schiller Institute: Because this is the only way, as I have experienced, to make a change in the world that has an impact on every living being on the planet.

So, now, with the World Land-Bridge we are many. We have whole nations also joining the New Paradigm, and we can all see that the prospect for a prosperous and beautiful future for all nations is within reach. Therefore, I urge every one of you, that in the midst of the worst suffering, we always have to have our eyes, not on the mud under our feet, but directed toward the bright stars above.

Thank you very much.

WANG HAO

A Role for Europe in The Belt and Road Initiative

Wang Hao, in the Embassy of the People's Republic of China to the Federal Republic of Germany, is First Secretary for Economy and Trade. He spoke on Panel II of the Schiller Institute conference, on June 30, 2018.

Good afternoon, everybody! It's a great honor to be invited to attend today's meeting. First of all, I'd like to extend my sincere thanks to the Schiller Institute, which has put a lot of effort and passion—in German, we say *Leidenschaft*—into organizing today's conference.

Wang Hao

My topic is "A Role for Europe in the Belt and Road Initiative." This is a topic which the organizers gave me. I found it a difficult, but a meaningful one. Difficult because, as a diplomat it is hard for me to tell Europe how it should engage in the Belt and Road Initiative. But, on the other hand, it is meaningful that, as the largest trade partner of China, the European Union should participate in this initiative.

European entrepreneurs have also shown their interest. So today, I would like to have a discussion with you regarding this topic.

Why the Belt and Road Initiative?

First, I would like to share with you why China put forward the Belt and Road Initiative. The spirit of the Silk Road was the connectivity of different peoples. In the age of globalization, this spirit still has its meaning. One of the preconditions to connecting people is infrastructure, such as roads and railways. China has learned from the imperialists how important transport facilities are for the development of the economy.

I would like to tell you a story of my own. When I was a kid, I often went to see my grandparents, who lived in the provincial capital, which was less than 200 km away, but travel took almost a whole day, due to the bad road conditions at that time. It was not only a waste of time, but also reflected the inefficiency of the economy. Nowadays, the two cities are connected by a highway, just like most other Chinese cities, and the journey takes less than two hours. We Chinese have a saying: "To get rich, you must build a road first."

Today, China is the second largest economy in the world, and building an advanced infrastructure network has made an important contribution to that. Presently, China has 136,000 km of expressways, and 25,000 km of high-speed railway, which accounts for two-thirds of the world's total. Seven of the ten biggest seaports worldwide are located in China. Both passenger and cargo rail are rapidly developing in China. All of which has changed people's lives, as well as laying a solid foundation for the rapid development of China's economy.

In the age of globalization, there are still many places around the world which are underdeveloped and lacking basic infrastructure. The needs in these areas are enormous. According to the Asian Development Bank, Asia alone will need to invest $1 trillion every year from 2017 to 2030 in infrastructure, in order to maintain its growth momentum.

As you might know, facilities connectivity is one of the five priorities of the Belt and Road Initiative. Here, facilities refers not only to transport facilities, but also includes oil and gas pipelines, grids, and cross-border cable construction. The aim is to expand road and rail links, and eliminate traffic bottlenecks to facilitate international transport and trade; and the improvement of ports and Asian infrastructure, oil and gas pipelines, grids, and cable networks.

We believe that proper transportation infrastructure is the basis for economic development. That is one of the reasons why China put forward the Belt and Road Initiative.

I would like to emphasize here that the Belt and Road is not a strategy, but an initiative. Every nation can participate and benefit from it. The Belt and Road Initiative is a public good that China offers to the world: It is a fast train to prosperity that is ready to take everybody along. It's also a massive, long-term project, not just for short-term profit.

Europe Is Already Benefitting

China is a country with limited resources and capabilities that depends on the active participation of other partners, including Germany and Europe: Here is how Europe can make a contribution and benefit from it. Actually, 19 European countries, including Germany, Great Britain, and France are members of the Asian Infrastructure Investment Bank (AIIB), which provides solid financial support for the Silk Road initiative. Germany is represented as the largest non-regional partner in the AIIB. Deutsche Bank belongs to the first group of non-regional financial service providers for the Silk Road initiative.

European companies also participate in projects within the framework of the Belt and Road Initiative, with their technology, capital, products, and know-how. I would like to emphasize that in order to participate in Belt and Road, European enterprises should take initiative themselves, instead of waiting for projects to come to them. They should look for the opportunities. In this area, the chambers of commerce of Europe in the countries along the routes can play an important role.

Ladies and Gentlemen: By cooperation along the Belt and Road, China and Europe both benefit economically and give the states along the routes improvement in both economic development and living conditions, which will further provide new opportunities for busi-

China-to-Europe rail freight. There were more than 3,000 fast-train trips between China and Europe in 2017.

ness and improve Europe's internal and external security.

We already have some visible achievements, such as the more than 3,000 fast trains that have operated between China and Europe in 2017—forty-eight of them between China and Germany. The fast train has become a symbol of the initiative in Europe. Duisburg and Hamburg are two important destinations in Europe and have benefitted a lot from it. Other cities, such as Mannheim, Rostock and Bremen have also shown great interest in operating fast trains. We encourage more European companies to use fast trains to export their goods to China and other Asian countries, in order to save time and lower costs.

Last but not least, I sincerely hope that Europe and China will go along with the trend of the times, engage in open and win-win cooperation, embrace reform and innovation, and seize the historical opportunity of the Belt and Road Initiative.

I must apologize for leaving early, and cannot participate in the panel discussion although I am eager to do so, but my colleague and I have to catch the train to go back to Berlin, because our prime minister will be visiting Germany in a week. So, there is a lot of work waiting for us.

I wish the conference success, and wish all of you a nice day. Thank you.

After the Transaqua Breakthrough, Nigeria Comes to the Fore

H.E. Ambassador Yusuf Maitama Tuggar, the Ambassador of the Federal Republic of Nigeria to Germany, spoke on Panel II of the Schiller Institute conference, on June 30, 2018.

Thank you very much! Let me begin by commending the organizers, the Schiller Institute, for hosting such a conference, which seeks to discuss something that the President of the Federal Republic of Nigeria, and I in particular, hold dear to our hearts, which is the inter-basin water transfer from the Congo Basin to the Lake Chad Basin.

When I was first invited, it was to a panel discussion, so I focused on simply having a discussion. The topic was to be, "After the Transaqua Breakthrough, Nigeria Comes to the Fore." I decided, instead of preparing a speech, to just stick to my discussion, which is what I'm going to do while I stand here, so I hope you will not mind that.

Inter-Basin Water Transfer to Save Lake Chad

The inter-basin water transfer, like I said, seeks to transfer about 100 million cubic meters of water per year from the Congo Basin to the Lake Chad Basin, and in particular to Lake Chad itself, which has been shrinking over the years. It has been the subject of international discussion, because it underscores what most of us are concerned about, which is climate change, desertification, conflicts, because it happens that the Sahara region, and the Lake Chad Basin area in particular, is an area where a lot of these issues are coming together. So it's the nexus for conflict, for migration, and for hydrocarbon exploration, because oil and gas have been discovered in Niger Republic, and in Chad. There are pipelines being built.

And of course, everyone knows about the Boko Haram conflict that was going on there. Thank God, it has been surmounted by the requisite collaboration between African countries, because the region happens to

Ambassador Yusuf Maitama Tuggar

be in one of the most complex cross-border areas in Africa, if not *the* most complex, where four countries meet: Niger, Chad, Cameroon, and Nigeria. One of the reasons why there was a lag or delay in tackling the Boko Haram problem was that there was a failure to define it the way it is, which is a cross-border conflict, and to use the collaboration of the countries in the region to solve the problem.

Now this, thankfully, changed when the current President, Muhammadu Buhari, was sworn in, in 2015. Five days after his swearing in, he embarked on a visit to Niger, to Cameroon, to Chad, and essentially said, "Look guys, we have to come together. We have to collaborate and solve this problem."

Now this was no fluke, because he happened to also be a former governor of Borno State, which was ground zero for this conflict, so he understood the region very well. And he knew that historically, going back to tackle such problems, such as the case of Rabih Zubayr in 1897, and other such cases, you needed the collaboration of all the countries. At least since 1964, there's always been an organ to tackle this sort of problem.

The water transfer issue is being spearheaded at the moment by the Lake Chad Basin Commission. Thank God, the foremost expert on this water transfer happens to be part of the panel, so I was happy to see his name there: Mr. Mohammed Bila. In fact, truth be told, he ought to have spoken before me so that I can just cruise after that, but be that as it may, I will do my best. But the technical details, the deeper insights into what is to be achieved, I'm sure he will explain.

China, Europe in African Development

I don't want us to look at this project, or indeed, other developmental projects that are going on in Africa, and in Nigeria in particular, through the binary lens of China versus Europe—the sort of binary approach that is perhaps some sort of Cold War lag, where we think that if

Schiller Institute

The Council of Ministers of the Lake Chad Basin Commission conference, February 2018.

China is playing, then Europe is out, or if Europe is playing, China is out. We need the cooperation, the collaboration of all three, because it's not just Europe and China either; Africa is also at the table and there is a need to ensure that Africa is always represented, and is part of the discussion that develops any solutions, be they infrastructure, development, migration, what-have-you, Africa needs to be a part of it.

One of the reasons why, with the Lake Chad issue, we need the full collaboration and participation of Europe, and not just China, is because this will be a part of the One Road, One Belt Initiative, which fits in *perfectly* with the concept of globalization, because it's about interconnectivity, which is the way we look at the world. This is what has happened over the course of human history. We have to redefine the map of the world, or the part of the world that we know, as we did before we even discovered that the whole world was a globe. So, we've gone from Terra Rugeriana, the Idrisi map which was actually upside down. He looked at it differently. So we also need to start looking at globalization, that connectivity.

We need to perhaps lay more emphasis on maps that highlight infrastructure lines, rail lines, transmission lines for electricity, roads, and so on and so forth, as opposed to more of the Halford Mackinder type of approach, which is to have a Eurasian World Island and then everything else beyond that is a Rim Land, it's a Shatterbelt; it's all of that. We need that collaboration, and the only way you can achieve these sorts of developmental and infrastructure leap-frogging initiatives in Africa is when you utilize the existing knowledge, the existing database.

And this is where Europe has a critical role to play, because, I have to say, it is for me, it's perhaps *kismet* that we happen to be holding this gathering in no less a place than Germany. Because some of the earliest irregular migrants that were received in the Lake Chad Basin area happened to be from Germany! It was Heinrich Barth in the 1850s, it was Gustav Nachtigal; it was his nephew (I forget his name now), a priest who did a lot of extensive studies of the flora and fauna, the culture and much more about the Lake Chad area. Perhaps there is a need to tap into all that knowledge and data that was gathered, to be able to transfer huge volumes of water from the Congo Basin to Lake Chad, which would completely transform the sub-region, if not the entire continent. With such a feat, you would generate electricity, you would provide water for irrigation, provide transportation and fishing activities—so much. Work would be provided for the teeming youth, who are always looking to make that desert crossing—so the issue of irregular migration would also be touched by such a project.

Quite a bit of ground has been covered. I remember when the President of Nigeria was sworn in. Shortly after that, I had a meeting with him, and I was emphasizing the need for the current administration to make progress on water transfer. I talked to him about the 1990s, when some of these efforts were initiated, and 2000, when on the legislative side in Nigeria, a committee was created that was meant to be a regional committee for the Lake Chad, to tackle some of the funding issues, some of the sensitive issues, so each member country would have two legislators representing them on the Lake Chad Basin Commission. He told me, "Look, I became involved in this and took up interest in this in the 1970s." This was when he was Petroleum Minister, when he flew with then President Obasanjo, and the Foreign Affairs Minister Joe Garba, to meet with Ahmadou Ahidjo in Cameroon.

So you see, it goes all the way back. It's something that needs to be done. These are the sorts of transformative projects that we need to be able to achieve what we keep mentioning, sustainable development. Sustainable development is not going to be achieved by simply listing goals. We need to identify these sorts of transformative projects, to fund them, support them, see them through to fruition. The only way that we will be able to achieve that is if we all put our hands together—hands and heads. So it's China, it's Europe, it's Africa.

Thank you very much.

MOHAMMED BILA

Looking Ahead: Will Africa Become the New China?

Mohammed Bila is an Expert Modeler at the Lake Chad Basin Observatory, Lake Chad Basin Commission. He spoke to the conference on behalf of the Commission.

Claudio Celani: So, now it's over to you, Mohammed. Mohammed Bila—we have known each other for three years now, and he is also a Nigerian. Don't think that Nigeria is over-represented here, because he represents the eight countries of the Lake Chad Basin Commission.

Mohammed Bila

Mohammed Bila: Thank you, Claudio. Distinguished ladies and gentlemen, the Lake Chad Basin Commission is delighted to be given this opportunity to interact with the Schiller Institute. I have to convey the apologies of our Executive Secretary. Due to some constraints, he could not come. That is why he sent me to portray the viewpoints of the Lake Chad Basin Commission to the participants of this conference.

I am a modeler for the Lake Chad Basin Commission; I have been there since 2002. So, all the developments that have been going on, even before 2002 within Nigeria,—I have seen the impact of the drying of Lake Chad. I have seen the attempts made by the different governments to solve the problem. I have seen the support that the international community has been giving to the Lake Chad Basin and the member states. But as of 2012, we had a totally different, new challenge, that is, an open conflict with people who feel they must change everybody. This problem, if we had looked for a solution 30 years ago, probably would not have reached this state.

The Congo-Lake Chad Inter-Basin Water Transfer became a solution to the problem of the drying up of Lake Chad, when the Eighth Summit of Heads of State and Government of the Lake Chad Basin Commission (LCBC), held in Abuja in March 1994, launched an international campaign to save Lake Chad. With the election of President Muhammadu Buhari in 2015 in Nigeria, and his appeal to the international community to help in recharging Lake Chad, to revive economic activities and reduce terrorism, the LCBC decided to look at one of the oldest proposals we had, which was called the Transaqua proposal. The proposal was developed in the 1980s as a comprehensive solution to the longest Sahel drought on record. It started in 1973, but in the 1980s, we still had this drought.

The Abuja Declaration of 2018

In March 2018, under the leadership of President Buhari, eight African heads of state and government came to Abuja to attend the International Conference to Save Lake Chad. Those eight heads of state, based on the proceedings and discussions in the workshops, chose the Transaqua project as the most viable option to save Lake Chad, but also to transform Africa.

In this meeting, we had the heads of state from the LCBC countries, five of them, and then we had a representative from the government of Libya, and also President Ali Bongo Ondimba of the Central African Republic of Gabon. We also had the affirmation of the proceedings of the conference by Denis Sassou Nguesso, the President of Congo Brazzaville; he called during the conference and said, "I give all my blessings to whatever comes out of this conference." So, this was the first time the African leaders came together and tried to look for a common solution that will solve the problem.

The Transaqua proposal consists of a 2,400 km waterway, to transfer between 30 to 50 billion cubic meters of water. The initial proposal that was done in the 1980s by the Italian engineer Marcello Vichi, thought we could get 100,000 billion cubic meters and move it to Lake Chad. But from then to now, we have been having a consistent drought, so the general thinking is that we might not get 100,000 billion cubic meters, but we can

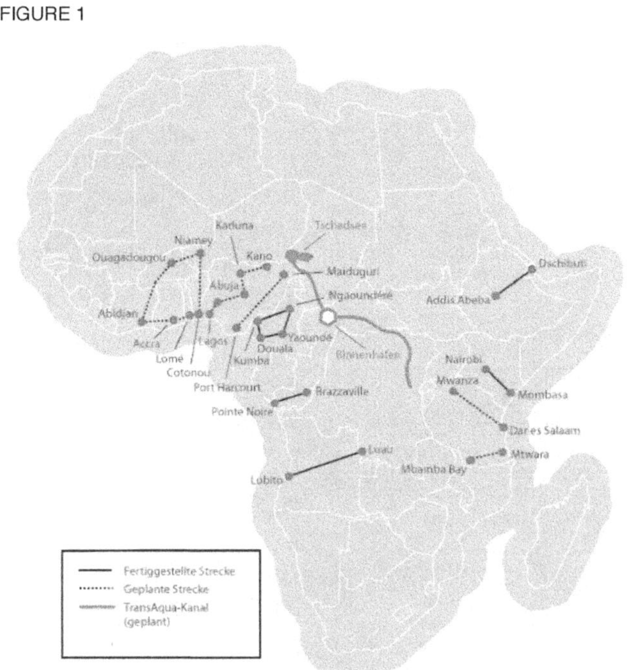

get between 30 to 50 billion cubic meters taken from the right-side tributaries of the Congo River transferred to Lake Chad. The project is expected to bring economic development to seven African countries and indirect benefits to five more countries associated with the Congo and Lake Chad basins.

At the end of the conference, the Abuja Declaration was endorsed by the Heads of State, in which they noted that the drying up of Lake Chad and the loss of sources of livelihood in the Sahel are affecting human security through southward migration and conflict towards Central Africa and Congo; insecurity of lives and property in the Sahel, the Lake Chad region, and West Africa in general; and negating the stability of Central Africa in the long term. So, this is a gradual thing.

Since 1973, those who have assets, that is, those who have cattle, have been moving away from the Sahel; they have been going towards the center of Africa. That is where the grass is green. They are trying to protect what little assets they have by moving southward. This migration is taking them to a new region where they meet people with different cultures, with different languages. This is the main cause of the problem in the Central African Republic. So, we have concluded that if we don't revive the situation, this southward migration within Africa will cause more problems in the regions that are already experiencing internal conflicts. Also, this loss of livelihood is costing the young in the Sahel region to move up north through Libya to Europe.

The Abuja declaration endorsed the Transaqua Inter-Basin Water Transfer initiative as a pan-African project necessary to restore Lake Chad for peace and security in the Lake Chad region, and for the promotion of navigation, economic development, and industrialization in the whole Congo basin. The African Development Bank was mandated to facilitate the creation of the Lake Chad Fund of U.S. $50 billion. The funding sources shall include a social component, funded through public sources from African states, and an economic component, funded using public funds and loans and donations by Africa's development partners.

DR Congo Will Be First to Benefit

This picture of the Transaqua project [**Figure 1**] shows the rail links needed to create the infrastructure [being built with help from China, independent of Transaqua]. The blue in the center is the Transaqua Water Navigation Canal, which will start in the south of the Lake Victoria area, the Lake Kivu region, which goes along the crest by gravity, reaching the Central African Republic, where we expect to develop an industrial zone. This canal will drop its water into the Chari River, which will gradually recharge the Lake Chad.

These are the regions that will be impacted by this Transaqua Project. [**Figure 2**] You can see that the first

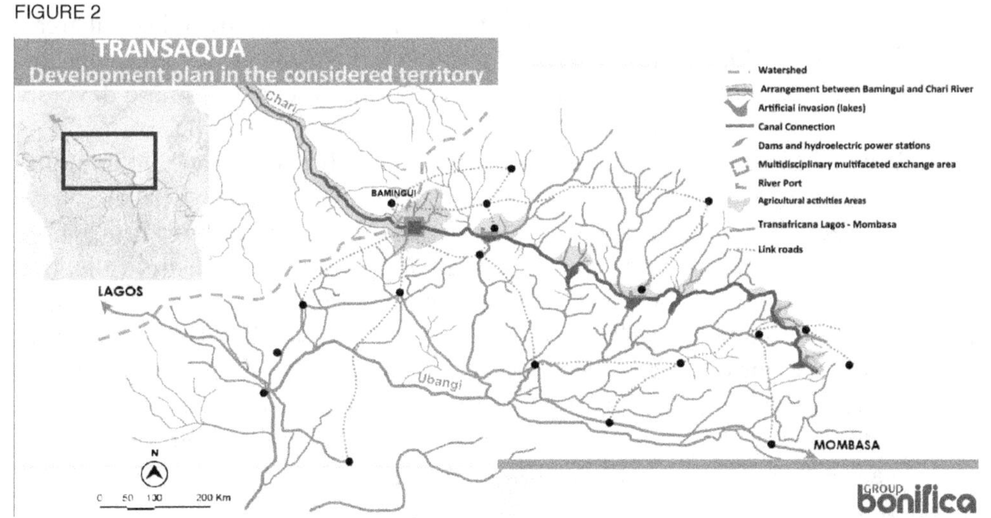

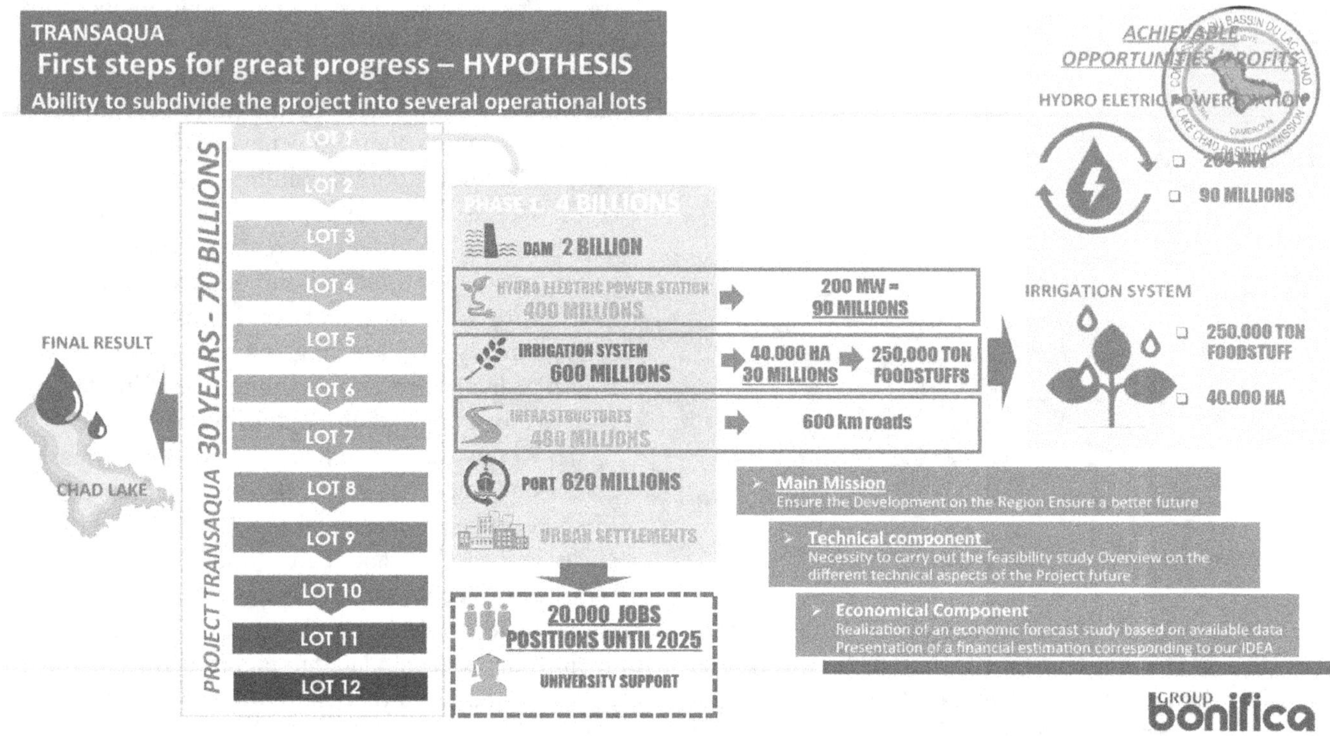

beneficiary will be the Democratic Republic of Congo (DRC), because the water will be generated from that basin. We need new concepts to describe what is happening. The traditional concept is, you take water and allocate it to a country or to a group of users. But with the new concept of having a benefit sharing, win-win situation, we cannot go with the traditional concept. So here, we foresee a certain stock of water, which has one value, taken from the Congo River, moving along the canal. It's adding value in transportation of goods; it's adding value by replenishment of that canal. This water goes into the Central African Republic.

When this stock of water moves, dams will be created. We have identified that at the tributaries, dams will be created. These dams will generate electricity; so this is another added value from this stock of water. And as it moves to the Central African Republic, the hydroelectricity could be used, and the water could be used for irrigation. This same stock of water will move into the Lake Chad basin across the divide. Cameroon can use the water for irrigation, the electricity already generated can be shared by Cameroon, can be shared by Chad, because these are all regions where we don't

have electricity. So these are all benefits that come out from this project.

Eventually, this water will go into Lake Chad. Niger is going to benefit from irrigation and whatever else they want to develop the water for. So, this is a big opportunity for movement of goods and services from central Africa to the Sahel, from the new irrigation projects. Instead of Africa *importing* billions of tons of rice every year, this project will be capable of generating that quantity of rice *within* Africa. The industrial areas, the container terminals that will be set up along this navigable canal, will bring in new economic development.

This stock of water will also revive biodiversity; most especially in the Congo Basin, where they have large protected areas—parks. When you bring more water into those areas, you enhance the multiplication of biodiversity in these protected areas. So this project will not only develop Africa, but it will also help us to revive biodiversity, protect the Central African Republic, and at the same time also revive biodiversity in the Lake Chad. It will boost regional trade, create new economic infrastructures, such as river ports, container terminals, agro-industrial zones and new

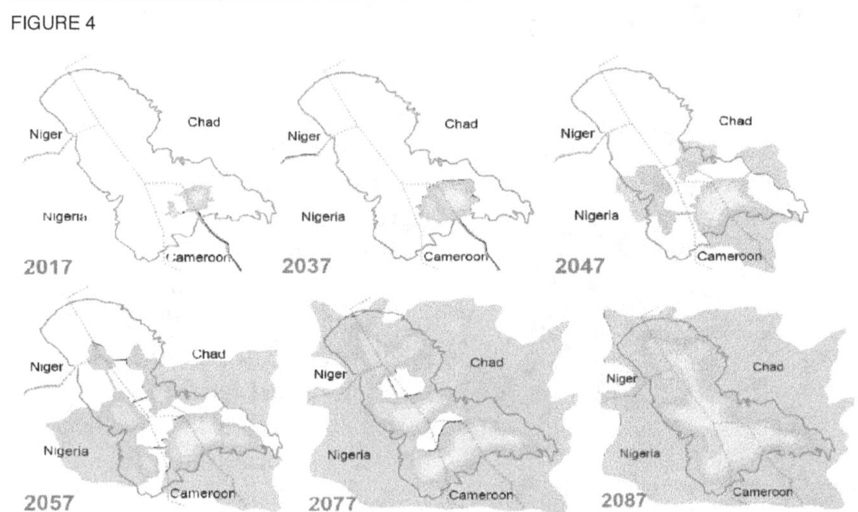

roads. There are areas where there are no roads. In the DRC, if you move from one town to the other, if it is not on the Congo River it is a hell of a challenge for the people. They have to go either on a bicycle or a motorcycle. These projects will definitely build new roads.

Financial Return from the Beginning

The project doesn't need to be implemented all at once. The company that we have been working with, the Bonifica group of Italy, makes simulations. Their simulation says we can break it down into as many as twelve phases. From the first "operational lot" [phase], we can generate economic goods; and from the money generated by selling those goods, we can proceed to the next phase, the next lot. So, gradually, the African countries will even have the capacity to plan it in such a way that they can call whichever partner they want to participate in developing the different lots.

The simulation says that generating financial returns immediately when we start the first phase, is capable of providing stable growth for the next 30 years— the expected duration to really complete the project. So, you have a constant inflow of capital, a constant financial result, which is taken into the next lot of the project. So, gradually the project will provide financial sustainability right from the beginning.

The first lot of the project, which Bonifica has simulated, is building a dam in the Central African Republic capable of generating 200 MW of hydroelectricity; development of four irrigation systems covering an area of more than 40,000 hectares; construction of up to 600 km of roads; building several new urban settlements; and building an industrial and logistical complex with the creation of the direct employment of at least 20,000 people and approximately the same number of jobs created indirectly. This is based on an investment of just about 4 billion euro. This result can achieved by 2025.

Nkrumah Had This Dream

So, if I can go back to the question, "Will Africa become the next China?" The answer is yes, if we make this investment in the Central African Republic, and we go ahead over the next 50 years—this partnership between Africa, Europe, and China. In 2016, China pledged to President Muhammadu Buhari to invest in this project. You are the first people who started the feasibility study to do it. Later on, we were so happy when Italy decided to join. During the conference in Abuja, Italy donated 2.5 million euro to the feasibility study. So, China has already invested $1.8 million, and now Italy has joined with 2.5 million euro. So we now have the ability to do a comprehensive study for the Transaqua project. It's much more than just a water transfer project; it's a transformation project for economic growth in Africa.

The realization of the Transaqua infrastructure project with the support and partnership of Europe and China will surely launch Africa on the road to economic growth, human security, industrialization, peace, development, and the attainment of the dreams of pan-African leaders such as Dr. Kwame Nkrumah. Nkrumah had this dream in 1964. If we start investing in this partnership now, in the next 50 years, Africa will become the New China.

We have mapped out the roads that will be created in just the first lot, in the Central African Republic, and what we expect Lake Chad to be in 2087 with the lake no longer broken into the different pools we have now. We will have a single body of water. We have mapped the potential area to be irrigated along and around Lake Chad in all the countries. We have the strong belief that this will transform Africa.

Thank you for your attention.

DR. AMZAT BOUKARY-YABARA

What Pan-Africanism on the Silk Road?

Dr. Amzat Boukary-Yabara, African historian, is General Secretary of the Pan-African League--UMOJA. He is the author of Africa Unite! Une histoire du panafricanisme *(Paris, 2014).*

Ladies and gentlemen,

I thank the organizers and the speakers at this international conference of the Schiller Institute, and Solidarité & Progrès, who asked me to intervene. This is the second time that I have the opportunity to speak with you here, in Germany.

I'm a historian and I intervene as Secretary General of the Pan-African League—UMOJA. Umoja means "unity" in the African language of Swahili. We are a political party, active in some 15 African countries, most notably in Congo, Ivory Coast, Mali, Niger, and Senegal. We are active also in the Diaspora: France, Belgium, England, Switzerland, and North America, and we have sympathizers in China and in Russia. The headquarters of our movement is in Cotonou, in Benin.

Our political orientation is the tradition of the "Prime Combat," the model for the United States of Africa,[1] which is aimed at making Africa self reliant in realizing its development by its own means. We aspire to restore to ourselves our own local and national governing aspirations. Our political program starts from the recognition that Africa is at the cross roads of globalization and of balkanization, and it must free itself through the following three steps : the conquest of power at the local and presidential level by progressive and pan-Africanist forces, the construction of a politically integrated Africa with its own values, and finally, the creation of international alliances collaborating with us in assuring that Africa will no longer be the the playground of world disorder.

Each one of these three stages must effectively investigate the necessity to search effectively for a new paradigm within international relations, because of challenges

Dr. Amzat Boukary-Yabara

which present themselves today in different forms such as, for example, the emancipation of women, which is a great African project, the ecological question, the demographical problem, the digital revolution, and the new domain of bio-technology, and in what we are very concerned about, us Africans, what I call the second phase of decolonization—because there has been a first phase during the 1960's generally, which was definitely not sufficient.

One China, One Africa

My intervention, therefore, is on the resolution of the equation posed by China to Africa: *What Pan-Africanism on the Silk Road?*

First of all, China is not a new actor in Africa. Around 1415, Chinese admiral Zheng He reached the coasts of East Africa during a period when the new silk road was about to be replaced by the Great discoveries and the route to the Americas. During more than five centuries, Africa was forced to open itself to all human and economic predations, in the context of slavery and of colonization.

China, on its side, shut itself off to the outside world before suffering the European and Japanese foreign occupations. In order to recover its own destiny, China first worked towards its political reunification with Mao's Revolution of 1949. The Bandung conference in 1955, the support for African national liberation movements and for the building of the Tanzania-Zambia railroad, showed that China, despite its geographical distance and the difficulties of linguistic communication, didn't wait to become a great power before coming to the help of the Africans during that first period of decolonization.

In the 1960's, several African countries recognized the People's Republic of China, including some French colonies before France did, for example, and supported China's return to the United Nations. Rather than looking to Europe and the United States for support, China engaged in South-South cooperation with the Group of 77 or with the BRICS, and even contested some of the rules of the WTO. Finally, China has no connection to

---

1. The idea of The United States of Africa (USA) was first coined by Marcus Garvey in his 1924 poem, "Hail, United States of Africa".

the structural adjustment policies which caused the collapse of all of the African states and economies in the last forty years. To develop herself, China never followed the Washington consensus or the IMF or World Bank directives.

However, the project for a New Silk Road policy in Africa brings responses, but also poses new questions concerning the Chinese presence. Let us be clear: China defends its interests and will develop its new Silk Road whether the West or Africans like it or not. Africa is the last frontier in that road, and the criticism espoused by the Western media against the Chinese presence in Africa is more motivated by the decline of the Euro-American influence in markets which they thought were going to be theirs forever, than by a real interest on the future of Africans for whom the question is not whether a new colonialism will replace a former one, but how to recuperate our sovereignty.

The first answer to those questions for Africa is that no development is possible without undergoing liberation and a revolution. We consider Pan-Africanism to be the movement which organizes African liberation and revolution. It's a political, economic, cultural, and scientific revolution, in which development is not an ideology but a paradigm—the paradigm of unity. Since Chou Enlai, Chinese diplomacy opened spaces in Africa relative to this paradigm of unity. A last example of this is that of Burkina Faso which just broke diplomatic relationships with Taiwan and announced that all projects previously entrusted to Taiwan have been taken over by Beijing. Indeed, the major condition that China poses in its partnership is that of recognizing the principle of One China. Pan-Africanism is also based on the principle of a "One Africa." One China, One Africa.

After Humiliation, Reparations and Reconstruction

In the present state of affairs, relations between China and Africa are not equal since China is a State-Continent and Africa is a continent of some fifty states of which none is equal to China, in spite of the potentialities of the territories like Nigeria and the Democratic Republic of Congo. When China, or another actor, negotiates with an African country, the Africans must negotiate with the general interest of all of Africa in mind. For that, every country must have a national policy which is complementary to a continental policy. In theory, it is up to the African Union (AU) to enable a collective response, but this institution, whose headquarters is located in Addis Ababa and which was built by China, has no supranational authority. The African Union has structural weaknesses such as its financing by the West, and the fact that it does emanate from the sovereignty of the African people. Nor is it in phase with the real political aspirations of Africa. If China, like Europe and the U.S.S., has an African policy within the context of the Forum for the Chinese Africa Cooperation (FOCAC), Africa has no Chinese policy nor a European or American policy. Africa has no solid relations, either people to people, company to company, civil society to civil society, or political parties to political parties. Only Pan-Africanism can therefore fill that gap.

The second point touches upon the question of reparations, a struggle carried out relentlessly by Africa, in vain, towards those political, military, financial, and religious actors who enriched themselves through the centuries of slavery and colonization. China is also demanding reparations from Japan for the massacres committed during the 1937-1945 occupation: the rape of Nanjing, the bacteriological experiences on civilians, the Chinese women violated by the Japanese soldiers.... So long as China was weak, Japan refused to face its own criminal past. Today, China has become strong, and imposes on to Japanese historians the necessary revision of their national history as a precondition to all negotiations, including the lifting by the Chinese of their veto against Japan's demand to have a permanent seat in the UN Security Council.

The Chinese and the Africans alike suffered from occupation and colonial humiliation. The Western museums are full of objects stolen from Africa as well as from China, and they have also invaded the African art market. For example, the Japanese sanctuary of Yasukuni is to Chinese-Japanese relations, the equivalent of the Island of Gorée to Euro-African relations. Last month, the Senegalese authorities renovated, with financial help of the European Union, the Europe Plaza in Gorée, an island which was a European slave herding center during several centuries. Not a single word was mentioned about this past slavery. The example of China towards Japan shows that the honor of a people lies in the defense of its history and its national heritage. The refusal to admit facts which are certain and duly established, because of quibbling, is contrary to true history. This is why Africa must be intransigent with historical truth.

Africans Must Decide

China is also part of the African Development Bank and of the Caribbean development bank. However, the priority for Africans and Caribbeans is to establish a Pan-

African Bank for reparations and reconstruction. That Bank must be built upon a revolution of the present financial system. In that system, the dollar and the European currencies which are backed by the Euro-American military industrial complex, which is engaged in a fight against the CFA [two currencies in the former French colonial sector which are guaranteed by the French Treasury] front, are dominant. Africa cannot, therefore, involve itself in a project which includes Europe and the United States under such conditions. This is why within the Pan-African milieu we believe, in all modesty, that the New Silk road should not include Europe in its neo-liberal and neo-colonial form. It would be unconceivable for the African civil societies to have to participate in an alternative project with forces which have dominated them historically. China is building corridors for its own development. The Westerners control areas for their own stability, and the Africans have less and less maneuvering room even if opportunities could be numerous. A Silk Road along which Africa sells its resources to China who resells them back to Africa as manufactured products, is not an equal to equal system, or is not a win-win partnership. It's the reproduction of a colonial mechanism with the Chinese multinationals replacing the Euro-American multinationals.

In that context, what are the real markets that Africans can keep in Africa and look forward to gaining in China? I don't see any, so long as we do not write in our constitutions our commitment to the transformation in Africa of raw materials into manufactured products in order to build an internal market which will meet its own needs. The point is for us to decide what goods we intend to put into circulation on the highways and on the railroads and which will be delivered across the integrality of the African continent. So long as Africa will not have made its economic revolution, it will never be an equal to equal partner of China, of Europe, or of the United States. We defend a pan-Africanist political economy where the rates of growth would correspond to real opportunities for the African people. China's capacity to mobilize its diaspora in order to avoid depending on foreign aid must inspire Africa to mobilize its

Senegalese scholar and scientist Cheikh Anta Diop in 1960 called for industrialization, nuclear power, and the highest levels of education.

own diaspora for its own financing. To achieve that, we recommend a strong approach to development for Africans and by Africans and not the sentimental approach of charity. Development is a question of interest which does not allow any room for capriciousness.

The Purpose of Infrastructure

The infrastructure projects financed by China are not projects initially conceptualized by the Chinese, but by the Africans. Since the 1960's, several African countries had plans to develop based on infrastructures construction, roads, bridges, hydro electrical dams, and factories of production. At the continental level, for example, we can talk about the Action of the Lagos Plan of 1980. The African countries were also competing between East and West to get material or financial support. Ideology was then a tool for development. When the West was conditioning aid to liberal governance criteria, China was showing that the liberal democracy model was not necessary to develop and invest in Africa. Starting in the year 2000, China invested in Africa, responding mainly to the requirements of African governments and of the AU concerning great infrastructure projects.

In reality, Chinese investments in Africa are very weak compared to Chinese investments in the rest of Asia or even in Europe, but they are sufficient to transform the situation. The moment China invests in a territory or in a sector which appears insignificant, they give it a real importance. Laying out a red carpet treatment, China values even the weakest. The African tours of Chinese officials enhance the African leaders while those of the French President are mainly humiliation sessions. [applause] A development plan cannot be reduced to financing infrastructure projects, but it is up to the Africans to put the content into the envelope. Do we want infrastructure at the service of the people or people at the service of infrastructure? What are we going to put on the Silk Road all across the African continent?

Cheikh Anta Diop Institutes

The question of language, science, technologies and environment is also central. The development of Confucius Institutes throughout Africa calls for a pan-African response via the Cheikh Anta Diop Institutes, named after that wise Senegalese who, starting from philology and anthropology, demonstrated the unity of African civilizations which goes back to Ancient Egypt, and who, in a book originally published in 1960 entitled *The Economic and Cultural Basis for a Federated State*,[2] presented an overall plan for the economic development of Africa and called for the teaching of an African language throughout the continent. The objective is to create a work language for Africa as a whole such that, for example, the work language between China and Africa would be neither English or French, but a language from Africa and one of China. This is a fundamental requirement. The working languages at the Organization of Shanghai Cooperation are Russian and Chinese. China has also been able to modernize its own economy and its international relations while keeping cultural elements which are part of its long history. Africa must also maintain this same sort of cultural requirement. [applause]

On the question of technology, China supported the access of Nigeria to space through the financing and launching of its communications satellites. In exchange, Beijing bought a share in Nigcomsat, the Nigerian federal communications company. For China, it's a matter of competing with the U.S.A. and Israel in the communications sector of Africa. For Nigeria, which is the first African power, it's a question of forming and training high level technicians which could make of that country the first African space power.

This is a vision which must be extended to the whole of the African continent, according to African interests, with the introduction of a true scientific program at the African Universities. In the 1980s , Burkina Faso president, Thomas Sankara, asked the USSR to train two Burkinaban scientists in order to enable the country to participate in the space adventure, which is the great adventure of mankind. Very much ahead of his time, Thomas Sankara was also preoccupied about the impact that space debris could have on the climate of a country like Burkina Faso, struck by draught and desertification. He had already observed a link between demography and the agricultural question, especially concerning the access to arable land around which there is today a new world competition on the African continent.

A Federal African State

The Pan-African development project takes into account both the necessary industrialization of Africa and the preservation of its environment, in the framework of achieving food self-sufficiency. Capitalism is no response to environmental challenges and thus the Paris agreement on climate is not an agreement for Africa. The principle of peace through environmental cooperation (environmental space building) would be a means to rethink the question of resources and of natural spaces which are, in general, across borders.[3]

Numerous African countries have launched emergency plans for the 2025-2030 horizon picking up on neoliberal and foreign recipes which have failed since forty years. This predictable failure of those emergency plans can only favor a process of re-colonization of Africa, so long as the struggles remain politically divided or absorbed by a system which maintains the illusion of a possible reform. An organized and disciplined revolution with demographic support cannot be avoided.

For the Pan-African League—UMOJA, the construction of a Federal African State must constitute the major objective of the African and Progressive organizations convinced of the odious character and the lack of future perspective of the world system now in place. China will probably dominate the world through its New Silk Road, and in that context the African resources will be more important for China than U.S. treasury bonds. Africa is thus the last border of world competition, but it can become—and this is our wish before the end of the century—the first world power if it works through its unity project in a sovereign way.

The responsibility is a heavy one. The task will demand years of work to get the results, but we are already engaged in a number of electoral processes from 2019 to 2021. The Pan-African league—UMOJA is a political movement. Before thanking you, we invite all the organizations and personalities present who are willing to contribute to our work, to make contact with us. "Umoja ni Nguvu," Unity makes strength. Thank you very much for your attention.

------

2. Cheikh Anta Diop, *The Economic and Cultural Basis for a Federated State* (Westport, Conn.: Lawrence Hill, 1974).

3. In 2011, Angola, Botswana, Namibia, Zambia, and Zimbabwe created the Kavango-Zambsi cross border conservation area (KaZaTFCA), the largest cross borders conservation zone on the entire planet. That type of project can be adapted to the Lake Chad basin or the Sahel region.

Challenges for Peace and Reconstruction in Yemen

This is a summary of presentations in German by two representatives of the Yemeni Association Insan for Human Rights and Peace (Germany). In Arabic, "insan" means "the human being." These presentations were a part of Panel II of the Schiller Institute conference, June 30, 2018.

Abdullatif Elwashali: Yemen has a young population. Unemployment used to be 37%; it is now 50%. The percentage of Yemenis living under the poverty line used to be 54%; it's now 85%. And these are not even up-to-date figures. There is a combination of epidemics, war and hunger. War: A coalition of 17 countries, led by the Saudis and the Emirates is attacking Yemen. The cause? To bring back the Saudi-backed President Hadi. After three years of war, our nation is destroyed, with 36,000 civilian casualties, including 14,000 deaths. Infrastructure is destroyed. We are under an air and sea blockade. Economic war is being waged against us.

Aiman Al-Mansor

Abdullatif Elwashali

Our financial situation is terrible. The health sector is destroyed, with 55% of medical facilities inoperable or destroyed; 1.25 million of our people are threatened by hunger and epidemics, and 896 of our schools have been completely destroyed. The hospital run by Doctors Without Borders was destroyed by air strikes in 2016, with dead and wounded, including the team of doctors. The worst case now is the port of Hodaidah. We are facing a humanitarian catastrophe, with 33 million people lacking even basic medical supplies. Food scarcity is the result of collapse of the financial situation. The ground water is collapsed. Humanitarian aid is not coming; the international community is reticent to help. The aggressors claim that they want to help, but no one here believes that.

Aiman Al-Mansor: The Saudis claim that they are helping, but what they are doing has nothing to do with democracy. They have destroyed our education. This is the greatest humanitarian crisis of the 21st Century. They want to weaken the Yemeni military forces, to force us to cede political control to the Saudis, and indi-

A classroom in Yemen.

rectly to the United States, as they have always done. They won't let the Yemenis decide. They want to use Yemen's geopolitical position to prevent win-win cooperation. Major economic interests are involved. The geographic importance of Yemen, is quite significant; it is now difficult to protect international commerce in the region. Before Yemen can be brought into the New Silk Road, we have to solve this grave humanitarian crisis. We need empathy from the international community. Saudi Arabia and the Emirates have to be convinced to leave Yemen alone. While the Chinese say, "To get rich, build a road," we say, "To participate in the international community, we have to end the catastrophe." This is a challenge to all of mankind, who can't be onlookers. We waited too long in Syria. Yemen needs new governmental institutions, new elections, and a reconstruction plan. The BRICS, China and Russia have to play an important role, to build their own peace initiative. The media needs to publish independent information. We need schools, roads, medicine, and empathy. React quickly. Don't wait for the UN to react!

HUSSEIN ASKARY

Operation Felix: Yemen's Reconstruction and Connection to the Belt and Road

Hussein Askary is the Southwest Asia Coordinator for the Schiller Institute. His just-published report on Operation Felix, in Arabic, was summarized in English in the Executive Intelligence Review *in its June 29 issue. Here we publish Askary's preliminary remarks before he turns to* Operation Felix, *as well as his conclusion, and we refer the reader to that written summary, rather than largely duplicate it with a transcript of the rest of his oral presentation.*

Yemen is, I think, the perfect case of turning tragedy into victory, a victory not only for Yemen or the Yemeni people, but for all mankind. And I will explain why.

For three and one-half years, as our friends have described, the Saudi war on Yemen, backed by Britain, the United States, France, and other countries, has brought with it many tragedies—but also many ironies. It showed that the apparently weak do not necessarily have to lose in the face of the mighty.

Hussein Askary

Yemenis, while admittedly being the poorest people in the region, have a deep sense of historical identity and a culture that goes back thousands of years into history. They are a proud people with a republican sense of freedom and a rough terrain that is very advantageous in defensive warfare. All these factors made them capable of resisting the Saudi coalition, backed by some of the most powerful military forces on the planet, for more than three years. But that was at a very, very high price, as we have seen.

Another irony is that right in the middle of the worst war and humanitarian crisis, some Yemenis—for the duration of the war—have been studying economics as defined by Lyndon LaRouche and the Schiller Institute, in order to find out how to build a modern economy and avoid the disasters of the past. They also have been studying the New Silk Road and want Yemen to join the Belt and Road Initiative and the BRICS. As I said in my opening remarks earlier, "to survive tragedy, you have to look toward the stars," that is, toward the future, and derive inspiration and courage from them to survive the current fight and pave the way to solving the crisis.

Here Askary presented a summary of Operation Felix. *His concluding remarks follow.*

In conclusion I would like to say that, in a June 6 seminar in Sana'a, I proposed that the "government there adopt this plan as a key component in any peace and reconciliation talks between the different Yemeni belligerent parties," and that this would be the mission of the future Yemeni government: That everybody agrees that this is what we want to do when we have peace.

As I say in the report, we don't want to reconstruct Yemen to what it was before the war. Because before the war, as we remember, Yemen was "the poorest country in the region." So, it's not our intention to bring Yemen back to what it was: We want to transform Yemen into the future. (applause)

At the same time, it's a means of motivating the international community to consider the absurdity of the continuation of this war. And it shows that the people controlling the government in Sana'a are not mere militias with power ambitions, but are statesmen with visions and knowledge. The responsibility to stop this genocidal war is upon every individual and every government in the world, today. The vision for launching a genuine reconstruction and development plan in Yemen is in harmony with the New Paradigm of cooperation in the world as expressed in this conference so far.

Thank you very much.

Greeting from Michele Geraci

Prof. Michele Geraci is currently Undersecretary of State in the Italian Ministry for Economic Development (Industry, Foreign Trade, Tourism and Fisheries). His greeting was introduced and read to the conference on June 30, 2018 by Claudio Celani.

Claudio Celani: Prof. Michele Geraci has been teaching economics in Chinese universities for ten years and is a strong supporter of the Belt and Road Initiative. He was eager to come to our conference, but was then called to serve in the new Italian government. It is Italy's—and the world's—good fortune, but a misfortune for us today. Just a couple of days ago, he gave an interview in which he emphasized two matters. The second of these was that one of his priorities will be to promote Italian cooperation with China to develop Africa as the only real solution to the migration crisis. (applause) His first was about the crisis of the Italian national airline company, Alitalia, which is facing bankruptcy. Lufthansa has offered to buy it. Geraci told his Italian audience that instead of selling it to our competitors, we should call in the Chinese as shareholders.

His message, which we received in Italian, is as follows:

Prof. Michele Geraci: I had been invited to the Schiller Institute conference before I was appointed to a government position, and I had been planning to participate. Unfortunately, government and institutional duties have prevented me from coming. Nevertheless, I wish you great success, and I am looking forward to receiving the proceedings of the conference.

INTIMATIONS OF THE FUTURE

Revival of Michigan Central Station Cracks Open Door to the New Paradigm

by Susan Kokinda

June 30—From the moment that Ford Motor Company Chairman Bill Ford, Jr. announced that Ford was buying Detroit's most famous ruin, the derelict Michigan Central Station, something happened in the city. A wave of optimism rippled through the population and extraordinary things began to happen.

Shortly after the official June 11 confirmation that Ford had purchased the building, the Henry Ford Museum received an anonymous phone call. The caller offered to return the large clock that had hung on the outside of the 18-story station and had been stolen (or perhaps preserved) during the years that the empty station was looted and stripped. According to the *Detroit Free Press*, the caller said "Please send two men and a truck immediately. It has been missing for over 20 years and is ready to go home. Thank you so much."

In subsequent days, further calls flooded into Ford, offering to return stolen or lost items from the train station. Architectural restorationists contacted Ford to offer help. Others offered donations. An article in the June 27 *Detroit Free Press* commented, "After all, Ford is a multibillion dollar company. And while this project is a Detroit treasure, the Dearborn-based carmaker didn't expect people to call and offer cash."

When the Ford Motor Company announced on June 20, that it would open the building to the public for three days, the response was so overwhelming (20,000 people registered) that a fourth day was added. This author

The Michigan Central Station.

stood in line for two hours on a Sunday afternoon, along with thousands of other very happy people, for a chance to see the interior of the station. While the media had spent the previous week whipping up the population against President Trump over "babies being torn from their mothers' arms," and while those lining up to see the station clearly came from every political persuasion and every walk of life, not a single "toxic" discussion was overheard. People were reminiscing about the station, comparing notes on which of the area's auto plants they or their parents and grandparents had worked in, and were imagining the impact the revival of the station would have in bringing thousands of new workers into the city.

The Unseen Hand

Immediately after Donald Trump's 2016 election victory, *EIR* founder Lyndon LaRouche stated that the Trump victory was not a domestic, American political event, but rather an extension of an international process of change sweeping the world. Similarly, the response to the revival of Michigan Central, whether those who were standing in line or returning artifacts knew it or not, is part of the advance of the "New Silk Road" paradigm spearheaded by China, supported by Russia, and potentially joined by Trump's United States.

The train station had become the most iconic symbol of the decline of the industrial heartland. Built in 1914, and designed by the same architects who designed Grand Central Station in New York City, the interior featured marble ceilings, tiled walls, Doric columns, and a classical appreciation of curved spaces. In the decades after its opening, which coincided with the $5 day and the development of the assembly line, Detroit's population tripled. Workers came through the doors of Michigan Central from across the country and from around the world. When World War II broke out, a new influx of workers poured through Michigan Central to man "The Arsenal of Democracy," while others shipped off to war through the station. As the post-industrial society took its toll on Michigan, the station was abandoned in 1988. The Moroun family, which purchased the building in 1996, allowed it to fall into such decay, that it became an international tourist attraction of what became known as "ruin porn."

Wikimedia Commons/Albert Duce

Interior of the Michigan Central Station, now under renovation.

Ford's plans for the renovated building (scheduled to be completed in 2022) include moving Ford's electric and self-driving vehicle operations into it, and leasing out the rest of it for offices, retail space, and apartments.

But something else is stirring.

As part of the ceremonies surrounding the station purchase and the public tours, Ford hung banners and projected large displays on the front of the station. The main theme was "Creating Tomorrow Together." The rotating displays showed various Detroiters reflecting on what the city needed. Most interesting, coming from an automobile company, was the following: "When I think of the future and infrastructure, it's really about having a mass transit system that's really efficient and really, really works." Another one said, "Detroiters engineer things, design things, and build things. That's not gonna go anywhere. It's not just our DNA. It's the landscape here, our infrastructure is made for this, and it's why we're still relevant and hopefully we'll always be."

'I Want a Train'

When I was in the station, looking at a small exhibit of the history of the station and the city, the lady standing next to me spontaneously blurted out, "this is a train station. We need trains." She then went on to describe all the local, regional, and national cities to which Detroit should be connected. When I commented that U.S. Representative Debbie Dingell (D) had said the same thing, she said "well, that's the first thing she has ever said that I agree with." Dingell had been quoted by local *Free Press* columnist Rochelle Riley as saying, "I've already been talking to everybody [about a train] That was John Dingell's (Dingell's husband and former Congressman) dream to have this. We need a connector regionally and statewide. We need a train west to Chicago."

Riley herself wrote: "So dear Mr. Ford, as you and your team who have given so much hope to the city's oldest neighborhood, to the state's largest city and to urban meccas everywhere, trying to get it right, we need one more thing: A train … I want a train."

A few days later, the Ford Motor Company announced that it would preserve the passenger tracks at the station, but stated that the question of restoring passenger service was a regional transportation issue, something that was not in the purview of Ford.

In reality, it is the purview of the nation. Only a national mission to shift the entire economic platform of the country to a higher level of energy flux density and relative potential population density from a "LaRouchian" standpoint, will fulfill the hopes now being expressed by so many. It is time to think much, much bigger than self-driving cars shuttling people from Detroit to Dearborn, or a passenger train moving at 90 miles per hour between Detroit and Chicago. Look at China's network of 20,000 miles of high-speed rail. Look at China's plans to upgrade to a network of magnetically-levitated trains. Think of the machine tool, materials, and power requirements of such a national network. Locate Detroit and the industrial Midwest in that kind of future, and one can properly conceptualize how to use a train station, and the skilled work force that will coalesce around it.

A Michigan LaRouche PAC organizer recently presented LPAC's pamphlet, "2018 Campaign to Win the Future: LaRouche's Four Laws for Economic Recovery," to a candidate for national office. When the candidate turned a page and saw a map showing the connection between Russia and North America at the Bering Strait, he pointed to the rail connection and said, "That has to go through Michigan!"

Now you are talking about a train station.

You're Human!
Do You Know What That Means?

by Robert Ingraham

by Robert Ingraham

PART TWO OF A SERIES

In this second installment we shall examine some of the frauds and misconceptions about the origins of the human species, as well as the galaxy-influenced crises which confronted early Man. We shall return to the subject of human progress in Part 3. Part 1 of this series may be found here.

II.—In the Beginning

June 30—Lyndon LaRouche, practically alone, has revived Plato's approach to examining the human identity. Throughout his lifetime, he has fought again and again, in the fields of economics, physics, and music, to provoke in people a recognition of what it means to be human, to investigate the relationship of human consciousness with the lawful anti-entropic nature of our developing universe. This is where we need to begin our present discussion.

This is not easy for people. Society tells you—daily, in numerous ways—that you are an animal, and that the only things which are real are what you can touch, feel, see, hear or smell with your senses. Many people rebel against this moral and intellectual straitjacket. They know there is something more noble to their existence—but they don't know how to grasp it, to articulate it.

What LaRouche has insisted, is that the human species is a *productive* species—that each human individual can contribute to a better future, and that this is manifested in the creation of new technologies and new scientific breakthroughs, as well as in contributions to the classical arts. It is also LaRouche who has insisted that the development of the power of mind is the only legitimate source of actual wealth, i.e., the physical and cognitive advancement of humanity. All of human progress has been born through human acts of discovery. This is called human productivity.

EIRNS/Stuart Lewis

Lyndon LaRouche receives a model of Mars on his 90th birthday.

This is where we begin our search for the origins and upward progress of human civilization.

The first vemeadrifiable evidence of what can conclusively be described as human culture is dated to about two million years ago (mya). This evidence does not lie in bone structure, DNA analysis, or similar paleontological data. It is to be found in the *use of fire*. It is with the appearance of the controlled use of fire for heating, cooking and other purposes that the presence of human beings is established irrefutably.

Fire is not a primitive *tool*; it is a *discovery*. Its mastery was a mental action whereby individual man learned not only how to create fire, but to deploy fire. This self-conscious and deliberate use of fire was an

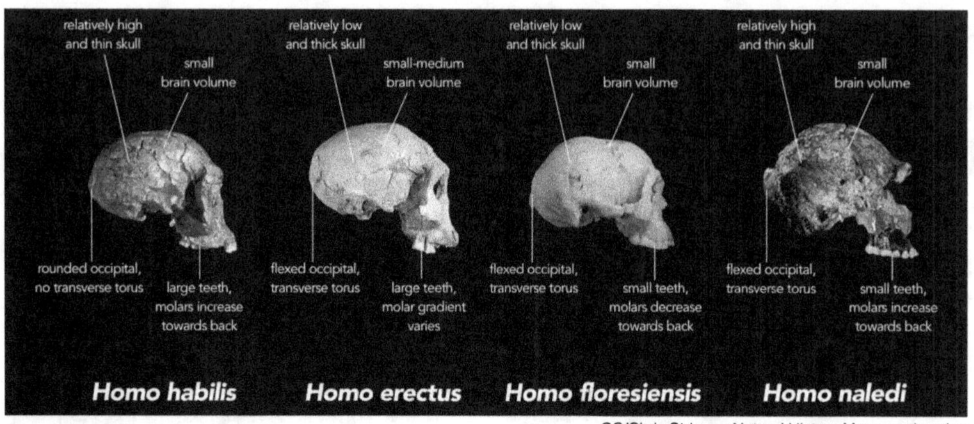

CC/Chris Stringer, Natural History Museum, London

Replicas of early human crania.

intervention into nature, one which initiated a transformation of the organization of the biosphere. It was the beginning of mankind's active *noëtic* role in the galaxy. At the same time, it unleashed a leap in humanity's productive power, uplifting our species and advancing human culture.

This is where human civilization begins.

Dispensing with Fraud

Before we go any further, we must first take out the smelly garbage which stinks up this entire field of enquiry. This begins with dumping the hoax known as "anthropology," a "discipline" that has been based almost entirely on works of fiction, ever since the sex-crazed Margaret Mead fabricated her stories about the Samoans. Controlled for more than a century from the universities of Oxford and Cambridge in Britain, the entire corpus of 20th and 21st century anthropological works belongs in the trash can.[1]

The next monumental fraud to deal with is the obsession by paleontologists and archeologists to define what they call "anatomically modern humans." This is what is taught in universities, and this is where the research money goes. The axiomatic demand of these professions has been to insist that the investigation into the emergence and development of the human species must be approached solely through the study of the human anatomy.

Simply put, these "scientists" do not comprehend what it is they are studying. They study human history as if they were examining the chronology of an animal species, and they demand that the development of the human species must be understood as entirely a physical biological evolution. But what defines human beings is cognition!—not their bone structure. The human species developed through the advancement of cognitive intervention. What no one in the academic world will recognize is that the human race is not a physically-determined species. We are not part of the Animal Kingdom.

These wizards of academia have devised an extremely elaborate lattice to give different names and classifications to what they call "pre-human" creatures (all members of the genus *Homo*). These include names

NYTimes Pictures/Jack Manning

Anthropologist Margaret Mead. Museum of Natural History, New York City, 1976.

---

1. Earlier, through the studies of Alexander von Humboldt, the work on language by his brother Wilhelm, as well as the writings of Joseph Herder, an actually rigorous approach to the study of human culture had been initiated, but this was almost universally supplanted in the 20th century by the imperial British outlook.

Painting by John Cooke, 1915

The Piltdown skull being examined. Back row (from left): F.O. Barlow, G. Elliot Smith, Charles Dawson, Arthur Smith Woodward. Front row (from left): A.S. Underwood, Arthur Keith, W.P. Pycraft, and Ray Lankester. The portrait of Charles Darwin watches over the huddle.

"archaic" humans, i.e., those individuals who "co-existed" for a time with Homo sapiens, including *H. neanderthalensis* and *H. denisova.* Most paleontologists insist that these people were not really human, and, again, these assertions are based entirely on anatomical differences with "modern humans," as if bones, or hair, or teeth determine what a human being is. Yet, it has been established that both Neanderthals and Denisovan Man utilized fire, built hearths, buried their dead, and therefore possessed language. In 2018, etchings and drawings in three Spanish caves were positively dated to 62,000 B.C., at a time before Homo sapiens arrived in Europe, thus establishing that what are labeled as "Neanderthals" possessed highly developed powers of cognitive imagination.[3]

This is all human culture! There is only one human species, a species which emerged as a self-aware expression of the cognitive living principle which is embedded in all of creation. The only legitimate issue to consider is the ongoing staggering advancement of human civilization, but to investigate the origin and development of the human race from that standpoint would require inquiry into the taboo subject of intangible human *noëtics.*

such as *H. habilis, H. antecessor, H. ergaster, H. rudolfensis*—and many more—all alleged "ancestors" of modern-day humans. All of this is based entirely on the study of bones.

Flow charts and arrows are drawn, comparing one bone to its alleged successor bone, thus defining a progression of "species." Careers have been made, and volumes written, based on very fragmentary evidence of fossil remains. These analyses all utilize a Euclidian mathematical methodology, and their findings resemble a computer print-out of inanimate data. In truth, the linear methods employed are identical to earlier efforts to find the "missing link"—the approach which led to the dupery known as the Piltdown Hoax.[2] It appears that these "professionals" have completely missed the point of James Weldon Johnson's *Dem Bones.*

There is also the case of what paleontologists label

The same axiomatic fixation on bones and anatomy comes up again in the study of *Homo erectus*, who scientists claim was the immediate "proto-human" predecessor of *Homo sapiens*, living from 2 mya to about 300,000 B.C. Again, it is insisted that *H. erectus* was "not human," and again, this is based on the skeletal differences with "anatomically modern humans."

But! If we define the self-conscious presence of creative Mind—not bones—as evidence of human existence, an entirely different picture emerges.

---

2. Piltdown Man was a fraud perpetrated by the British archaeologist Charles Dawson, who in 1912, claimed to have found the "missing link" between ape and man. It was not exposed as a forgery until 1953. Dawson had combined a human skull with the lower jaw from an orangutan and teeth from a chimpanzee, and had even filed the teeth into a shape more "human-like." Despite its eventual exposure as a hoax, today the *same fraudulent method* is used to base theories of human evolution on the development of bone structure and other physical characteristics.

3. In 2009, the Max Planck Institute released the "first draft" of a complete Neanderthal genome. They demonstrated that 1 to 4 percent of all modern non-African human genome comes from Neanderthals. Subsequent studies have placed the percentage of Neanderthal DNA in modern humans as high as 7.3 percent. This establishes irrefutably that *H. sapiens, H. neanderthalensis* and *H. denisova* (as other DNA evidence has shown) inter-bred, and since it is impossible for one species to procreate with another, what we are looking at is the development, over hundreds of thousands of years, of one human species.

Archaeologists Find Earliest Evidence of Humans Cooking With Fire

A cave in South Africa may be the site of the world's oldest barbecue — and a clue to early humans' development.

By Kenneth Miller | Tuesday, December 17, 2013

RELATED TAGS: ARCHAEOLOGY, HUMAN ORIGINS

Floodlights illuminate an archaeological site inside Wonderwerk Cave in South Africa.

Greatstock Photographic Library / Alamy

At the base of a brush-covered hill in South Africa's Northern Cape province, a massive stone outcropping marks the entrance to one of humanity's oldest known dwelling places. Humans and our apelike

Fire & Cognition

The earliest, as yet discovered, evidence for the human use of fire is dated to 1.5 mya, at the Wonderwerk Cave in the Northern Cape province of South Africa, where scientists discovered a massive cavern near the edge of the Kalahari Desert with evidence of both fire and cooked animal bones. Chinese scientists have also positively identified the use of controlled fire at the archaeological site of Xihoudu in Shanxi Province, dated 1.27 mya, and excavations in Israel suggest not only controlled fire but the construction of hearths. This is all within the era of *H. erectus* dominance.

Every living creature, other than man, hates and fears fire. It terrifies them. Yet as far back as 1.5 mya, human beings embraced fire as a means for survival during the brutal reality of the Quaternary glaciations. They went further, and learned to master its use for heating, cooking, and ultimately ceramics, metallurgy and the beginnings of physical chemistry. Man began to create his own environment, a human-directed environment. The use of fire, and its later improved use through the development of charcoal, and then coal, revolutionized man's relationship with the biosphere and the galaxy, as new inventions and discoveries vastly expanded the productive power of our species. This all flowed from human creativity. This is the Elephant in the Bed which no one deigns to see.

What the empiricists—and modern purveyors of information theory—insist upon is that there is no human *mind*; there is merely the physical brain, one which is biologically determined, and one which they view as essentially an organic version of a linear digital computer (After all, can't a computer beat a human being at chess?). What none of the atheistic materialists can answer, however, is the source of human creativity. This leads them into enraged outbursts against *metaphysics*, which they attack as "not-science." Yet it is precisely the metaphysics of Leibniz, Kepler and Cusa which is the true physics, for it explores the unseen non-material lawful principles which govern our universe. The human mind is the minimum of that maximum. The mind is not merely the physical brain. It is the cognitive soul of the human individual, acting in harmony with *agapic* creative universal principles.

The Challenge to Survive

Over the span of the last 2 million years, the earth, the solar system, and the galaxy have continued to evolve and change, all participants in an interwoven celestial dance. All of this greatly affected life on earth. The precise nature of these galactic processes is not yet understood, and research in this field is hampered by the hegemonic materialist Newtonian outlook. What is clear, however, is that the consequences of these transformations—over thousands of millennia—posed an ongoing threat to the survival of the human species. Tens of thousands of animal and plant species became extinct. Many animals, stronger and more agile than humans, vanished. The record presented immediately below gives some indication of the enormity of the challenge to human survival. Yet, the human species survived and ultimately flourished.

The beginnings of human civilization emerged during the early years of what is called the geological Pleistocene Epoch, a subdivision of our current Quaternary Period. The Quaternary Period, which is now about 2½ million years old, is defined as an ongoing ice age, one characterized by the advance and retreat of glacial formations. These processes have resulted in dramatic increases and decreases in both global sea levels and temperature, as well as formidable changes in the planet's biosphere. It didn't just get a little hotter or colder. Average temperatures could drop 10 to 15 degrees Celsius within five years, and the topography could go from alpine forest to Siberian tundra (or vice-versa) within decades.

During these two million-plus years, many other "natural" catastrophes are known to have taken place. There were several eruptions of "super-volcanoes" (the most powerful volcanic eruptions, with a Volcanic Explosivity Index [VEI] of 8), including in New Zealand, Argentina, and Wyoming. These were catastrophic events far beyond the explosive power of anything we have experienced in recorded history. There were also major galactic events, such as the Geminga supernova in 340,000 B.C. Astrophysicists hypothesize that the dazzling radiation from Geminga could have destroyed more than 20 percent of the earth's high-altitude ozone layer. Another supernova, Vela, exploded sometime between 10,000 to 20,000 years ago. About 800 light-years away, Vela is what is called a "near earth supernova," and is closer to Earth than any other human-era supernova event. At maximum light it would have out-shone the full moon. The radiation from this event would have affected humans—and the entire biosphere—worldwide.

In 780,000 B.C., the most recent, long-lasting magnetic pole reversal occurred and evidence indicates that there have also been more recent and more temporary magnetic pole reversals. North/South reversals of the earth's magnetic field are very interesting events whose causes and effects are still not fully understood. What is known is that the drawn-out process of a shift in the magnetic pole from north to south (or vice-versa) can take many years, during which the magnetic field of the earth may be significantly weakened. This could result in a sharp increase in solar radiation entering the atmosphere.

Milutin Milanković, Serbian Astronomer, as a student (1896-1902) in Vienna.

During the last glacial period there were two more super-volcano eruptions: at Lake Toba, Indonesia about 72,000 B.C., and the 24,500 B.C. Oruanui eruption in New Zealand. The Toba eruption deposited an ash layer approximately 15 centimeters thick over the entirety of South Asia, and as far away as the Arabian Sea; it is credited by some with creating a world-wide "volcanic winter." A number of scientists have even posited that its effects created what they term a "bottleneck in human evolution."

Current evidence indicates that this still-ongoing 2 million year ice-age has proceeded through 100,000-year cycles, consisting of roughly 90,000-year periods of advanced glaciation, interspersed with warmer 10,000 to 15,000-year interglacials. It is possible that these cycles are related to changes in the eccentricity of the earth's orbit, as posited by the Serbian astronomer Milutin Milanković. All of recorded human history has taken place within our current interglacial (Holocene) period, which is now approximately 11,000 years old.

Since the written record of human history goes back fewer than 10,000 years, people tend not to think in terms of 100,000-year cycles, or cosmic or volcanic events that happened hundreds of thousands of years ago. Yet all of these things occurred, and the impact on the earth's biosphere and all living creatures was severe. This continual advance and retreat of the glaciers, the change in sea levels, climate, solar and cosmic radiation, ocean currents, topography, and vegetation had a profound effect on all animal and plant life on earth. Tens of thousands of plant and animal species died off, including the vast majority of non-African mega-fauna (large mammals). In many areas, all of the dominant plant and animal species became extinct, and this process has continued into our current Holocene Epoch.

Yet, the human species survived, advanced, colonized three continents, and increased in numbers.

To be continued.

MARCH 5, 2001

The FDR Economic Recovery: Precedent and Practice

by Lyndon H. LaRouche, Jr.

The following is the advance text prepared for delivery at EIR*'s conference in Berlin on March 5, 2001.*

As we plunge into the worst global financial crisis in more than a century, only among those three national powers which were principal victors of World War II, the British monarchy, the United States, and Russia, do we find the historically defined, cultural temperament needed, to lead the introduction of a desperately needed, new world economic order for the planet as a whole. Only in two of those three, the U.S. and Russia, do we find any inclination among leading political institutions, to look back to the successful U.S. recovery policies of the 1933-1945 Roosevelt era, and to the 1945-1965 reconstruction of western Europe, as the basis for challenging the rampant follies practiced under the present IMF and World Bank systems.

Otherwise, among the NATO members of continental Europe, there has been, heretofore, a prevalent disposition to capitulate, however reluctantly, to policies situated within the post-1989 conditionalities, such as "free trade" and "globalization," which the presently incumbent Anglo-American authorities may choose to dictate to the planet as a whole.

Inside the U.S. itself, despite the efforts of my own and some other leading Democratic Party circles, to prevent such a catastrophe, there is, realistically, the increasingly awesome likelihood, that the present, Bush, administration, like the *Ozymandias* of Shelley's famous poem, might be stubbornly doomed to a self-induced, early, imperial disaster. Certainly, only madmen within the U.S.A. would wish such a catastrophe to occur, but only wishful thinking would mislead any leading circles, in any part of this planet, into believing, that a self-inflicted doom of the present U.S. administration is not a probable, catastrophic outcome at this present moment.

Meanwhile, among those inside the crisis-stricken U.S.A., and, to some degree, Russia, who see an onrushing global financial collapse now in the making, there is an historically deep-rooted, and commendable tendency, to think about the present world financial catastrophe, in terms of the contrast between the Franklin Roosevelt legacy and the contrary U.S. economic policy-trends of the past thirty-five years. Such views are also to be found today in western continental Europe.

For those and related reasons, for the foreseeable period ahead, the 1933-1945 Franklin Roosevelt recovery in the U.S.A., and its application to post-war cooperation between the U.S. and western Europe, represents *the only workable recovery policy with any chance of being adopted as a leading legal precedent for that quality of cooperation which might provide a timely response to the presently accelerating world financial collapse.*

Therefore, if the United States were to come to recognize, that it must reverse its current policy, and must prepare to cooperate with leading nations of Eurasia, in launching a recovery based on the principles which account for the successes of 1933-1965, the combination of the U.S.A., continental Europe, and keystone na-

There is also the case of what paleontologists label "archaic" humans, i.e., those individuals who "co-existed" for a time with Homo sapiens, including *H. neanderthalensis* and *H. denisova.* Most paleontologists insist that these people were not really human, and, again, these assertions are based entirely on anatomical differences with "modern humans," as if bones, or hair, or teeth determine what a human being is. Yet, it has been established that both Neanderthals and Denisovan Man utilized fire, built hearths, buried their dead, and therefore possessed language. In 2018, etchings and drawings in three Spanish caves were positively dated to 62,000 B.C., at a time before Homo sapiens arrived in Europe, thus establishing that what are labeled as "Neanderthals" possessed highly developed powers of cognitive imagination.[3]

This is all human culture! There is only one human species, a species which emerged as a self-aware expression of the cognitive living principle which is embedded in all of creation. The only legitimate issue to consider is the ongoing staggering advancement of human civilization, but to investigate the origin and development of the human race from that standpoint would require inquiry into the taboo subject of intangible human *noëtics*.

Lyndon LaRouche speaks to the Berlin seminar.

EIRNS/Christopher Lewis

tions of Asia, would represent a sufficient basis for bringing about the kinds of reforms which are now urgently needed by this planet as a whole. There is, presently, no other happy option available to this planet as a whole.

Admittedly, the recently installed U.S. Bush administration, seems absolutely determined to go in directions which are, chiefly, directly opposite to what I propose. Granted, that administration might maintain its present track in policy-making, up to what would be an extremely bitter end for the world at large. As the institutions of the U.S. will now experience more and more onrushing crises, far worse than they would presently believe possible, the present U.S. government attitudes might be changed, even suddenly. That change, if it is to occur, will either come soon, or the worst result for the planet as a whole is to be expected as more or less inevitable.

There is no possibility, no circumstance under which the present economic-policy outlooks of the U.S. administration could succeed. The early, absolutely catastrophic failure of those policies is absolutely inevitable; the signs of such a collapse are being displayed daily. However, like a maddened bull elephant in its death-throes, a desperate U.S. government's efforts to offset its economic failures with combined domestic and global crisis-management methods, could plunge the entire planet into homicidal chaos.

When we, in the U.S.A. and Europe, contrast the lessons of the Roosevelt economic-policy legacy of the 1933-1965 interval, with the growing world financial and economic disaster wrought over the recent three decades, there is a clearly urgent need to abandon those recent policy-shaping trends, and to return to the Roosevelt alternative, instead. However, that Roosevelt precedent, by itself, while indispensable, is not sufficient.

There is probably no effective substitute for the use of the successful features of the Roosevelt legacy as *a legal and diplomatic precedent* for the international emergency action so urgently required today. However, we must also be aware of the risks we would incur if Roosevelt's achievements were degraded to a mere caricature of itself, degraded to a mere model of a statistical type. Those risks are the focus of my attention here.

Precedent or Principle?

One of the most common blunders among professional economists today, is their attempt to explain the present crisis by treating it as if it were a cyclical, rather than a *systemic* crisis. This is not a periodic crisis; it is a breakdown caused by the wrong-headed, popularized axiomatic assumptions built into policy-shaping of monetary authorities, leading banking institutions, and governments, over a period of more than thirty years. No systemic crisis, such as this one, can be competently described, or controlled by today's commonly taught statistical methods.

As the founder of modern astrophysics, Johannes Kepler, said of the orbit of the planet Mars, the Roosevelt economic policy worked, and was certainly better than any alternative adopted since. Yet, whenever we think of past or possible future consequences of an asteroid crashing upon the Earth, we must recognize that some apparently regular trajectories of a solar system, or of national and world economies, may conceal some awesomely deadly systemic features easily overlooked by mere statisticians.

As Kepler did, we must look into the deeper principles which actually govern an observed past experience within our Solar System. It is not sufficient to try to imitate the successes of some observed period from the past. We must discover and apply the underlying principles which made an earlier success possible. We must also anticipate the danger of thinking simplistically about such matters. Asteroids, which apparently lie in a very reliable orbit, as do some economic-statistical models, sometimes crash on Earth, with horrible effects.

As Franklin Roosevelt explained, the methods which he applied to the aftermath of the 1929-1933 World Depression, were the methods of that *American System of political-economy* shared between Alexander Hamilton and a key Hamilton collaborator, FDR's ancestor, Isaac Roosevelt, in the opposition to one of the two leading U.S. assets of the British Foreign Office's of that time, the Bank of Manhattan's Aaron Burr. (The other was Albert Gallatin.) As Roosevelt emphasized, during his years as a university student and, later, as President, he located himself as a representative of the founders of the United States, and in opposition to what Roosevelt himself described publicly as those "American Tories" who were, in fact, typified by such predecessors as Presidents Theodore Roosevelt, Ku Klux Klan fanatic Woodrow Wilson, and Calvin Coolidge.

Roosevelt was born, raised, and walked in the American intellectual tradition of Presidents James Monroe, John Quincy Adams, and Abraham Lincoln. He, like economists Alexander Hamilton, Friedrich List, and Henry C. Carey, was a principled, and vocal opponent of the American Tory tradition. As President Abraham Lincoln defeated the virtually treasonous American Tory legacy of the Democratic Party of 1829-1861, so Franklin Roosevelt, a publicly avowed representative of the American intellectual tradition, reversed the catastrophic effects of the economic policies of American Tory President Calvin Coolidge.

During the entire period he was President, Roosevelt dumped, and also denounced, what he condemned as the "Eighteenth-Century methods" of the British monarchy. He rejected the notion of a post-war world under the rule of the methods of Adam Smith, and, during the course of World War II, proposed to introduce the American methods of Hamilton, List, and Carey, to a post-war world suddenly liberated of the vestiges of Portuguese, Dutch, British, and French colonialism.

The American Intellectual Tradition

In order to avoid the dangers of a simplistic imitation of the Franklin Roosevelt legacy, one must recognize it as an imperfect, but successful, remedial application of the American intellectual tradition in economic policy. By American intellectual tradition, I signify the Classical European tradition of Gottfried Leibniz's influence on the U.S. Declaration of Independence and the economic policies of Hamilton. I signify the repeatedly successful application of what Hamilton, Mathew Carey, Friedrich List, and Henry C. Carey defined as the "American System of political-economy." This was the same American System which, from 1877 on, played a crucial role in Bismarck's launching of the industrialization of Germany, and the industrialization of Russia under leaders such as the great Mendeleyev.

The commonplace, potentially catastrophic blunder made by many economists and others today, runs as follows. They would say, "If the economic crisis is as bad as you say, then, perhaps, we would then consider adding some amendments to existing policies." It is precisely that kind of popularized, simplistic, statistical thinking, which has done so much to mislead the world into the present economic mess. *We must cease the absurd practice of applying the statistical theory of kinematic percussions among inanimate objects, in the attempt to explain away the willful collective behavior of living human beings.*

The behavior of economies, as measured over a generation or longer, is chiefly predetermined by the long-term investments, and related long-term policies, made by governments and private interests, over periods of not less than a generation yet to come. By long-term policies, one means the intentions of society to invest with accompanying *intention,* that those investments shall become successful ones. These *intentions* are expressed not only as financial investments, but, as long-term physical investments in the future development of the population, the land-area, the fostering of scientific discovery, and the instruments of production. Like even the mere existence of today's young adult, today's conditions are the result of *intentions* expressed by that person's parents, about a quarter-century earlier. The only sane government, and the only sane form of economy, are those with sane *intentions, which commit the actions and resources existing in the present to the aims of the future.* These are economies like the U.S. economy under Lincoln and Franklin Roosevelt, and Fifth Republic France under President Charles de Gaulle, which are sometimes called *dirigist*, because of the clarity and efficiency of their economic *intentions*.

It was, chiefly, the *intentions* set into place, as policies and policies of practice, over the recent thirty-odd years, which created the cumulative effects being experienced as the global financial collapse of today. Today's crisis is not the result of some statistical theory; it is the result of wrong-headed *intentions*, such as the *intention* to impose free trade, and the *intention* to globalize the spread of such commodities as deadly diseases of human and animal populations. Today's crises are the result of *intentions* which have been adopted by governments, financial institutions, and popular opinions, over a period of not less than the past three decades. Inside the U.S.A. itself, today's crisis is the natural outcome of the trends introduced, since the 1966-1972 changes in direction of U.S. policy-making, trends typified by the growing influence of the Mont Pelerin Society and by the *pro-racist intentions* of the U.S. President Nixon who perpetrated the terrible folly of August, 1971.

As Kepler showed, the orbital pathway of a lawful trajectory of non-uniform curvature, is determined by what must be adduced as its *characteristic intention*. For the same reasons, the only valid assessment of a *systemic* financial-economic crisis, such as the present one, requires that we define that crisis, not as an inevitable calamity, but, instead, define those principles which require that we should *intend* to return to that trajectory which would lead to the imperiled system's survival.

Instead of debating whether or not we today should blindly imitate the programs of Franklin Roosevelt, we should examine his intention in introducing those programs, and contrast his *intentions* with the *intentions* of the faction behind President Coolidge's creation of the depression which the impossible Coolidge bestowed upon his own immediate, and unfortunate successor, Herbert Hoover.

Roosevelt did not propose a package of policies for responding to a depression. Roosevelt used the failure of Coolidge's economic policies, which were modelled on those of Britain, as proof that we must return to that American patriotic policy-making philosophy, whose violation had caused the crisis. He used the most recent failure of the British free-trade system, that of the 1920s, as evidence of the need to return to the superior philosophy of the American intellectual tradition and its *intentions*.

Today, we have the fact of the process of recovery of the U.S. economy from the Coolidge "free trade" philosophy's depression of 1929-33. We have the success of Roosevelt's return to the methods of the American System over the interval 1933-1945, and the application of that experience to rebuilding war-torn Western Europe during the 1945-1965 interval. Now, we have thirty-five years of the United States' slide into the present, new depression, a potentially bottomless depression, caused by the return to not only the "free trade" policies of the Coolidge period, but wildly utopian policies which are even far worse than Coolidge's.

The challenge facing us today, is to use the evidence that the ruling *intentions* of the world's leading economic policies, over the recent thirty-odd years, have been a catastrophe for mankind today. This evidence must prompt us to change the *intentions* of governments and other relevant institutions accordingly. We must now do, as Franklin Roosevelt did in response to the 1929-1933 Depression. We must clear away those policies which, as *intentions*, have brought about our ruin, and, install, instead, those *intentions of law* which correspond to proven principles of policy-making from successful earlier times.

That means, in first approximation, those *intentions* which have proven their merit during periods of modern history prior to 1965.

'The General Welfare Clause'

The crucial political issue separating President Roosevelt's recovery policies from those of all of his opponents, whether President Coolidge, his political opponents during his Presidency, or those from President Nixon to the present day, is what is called "the general welfare clause" of the Preamble of the U.S. Federal Constitution.

For as long as he was President, Roosevelt won most, if not all of his struggles to base the entire policy of the U.S.A. on that Constitutional principle. Since Republican Richard Nixon's alliance with the Ku Klux Klan and kindred types, during his 1966-1968 campaign for election as U.S. President, no President but Bill Clinton, has offered any significant defense of that principle, and he, during Summer 1996, compromised that principle, under maniacal demands from his Vice-President, Al Gore, and others among my political adversaries within the Democratic Party.

This issue of the general welfare, is the most crucial of all of the economic-policy issues which we must intend to confront if we are to succeed in rescuing the world by the presently onrushing catastrophe. The present, global economic disaster, must be traced to a persistently recurring effort, over the course of the Twentieth Century, to reverse the course of the entirety of modern European history, by going back to the imperial models of ancient Rome, to the traditions of the Venice-orchestrated anti-nation-state wars of the Thirteenth through Fifteenth Centuries, and the Venice-orchestrated religious wars of the interval 1511-1648.

Today, we call that revived, pro-oligarchical *intention* to return to medieval society, "globalization." The characteristic effect of the practice of what is called "globalization," is a rejection of any rule of law which opposes the effects of globalization, and demands a sweeping, global nullification of the principle known by the terms, *the general welfare* and *the common good*. To understand that issue, we must understand its origins and location in the history of today's globally extended modern civilization. The following historical background is a bare summary of what is essential for understanding the relevant connections.

As a reaction against the horrors of both the so-called New Dark Age of Europe's Fourteenth Century, and the continuation of the so-called Hundred Years War into the middle of the Fifteenth Century, the Fifteenth Century produced the antidote to feudalism known as the modern sovereign nation-state. This new form of society emerged first in the form of France as reformed by King Louis XI, and, following that, the great reform conducted under King Henry VII in England. These developments of the Fifteenth Century, established the beginning of modern economies, and the great improvements in demographic characteristics and conditions of life of populations which have resulted from the influence of that new, nation-state form of society.

The central feature of the revolution called the sovereign nation-state economy, was the introduction of a principle known as *the general welfare*, or *common good*. This new principle was the *intention*, that *no government has the legitimate moral authority to rule, except as it is efficiently committed to promote the general welfare of all of the living and their posterity*.

So, the law lies not in its text, but in the effective expression of its *intention*. So, by their intentions, do economies, and even entire civilizations, choose their destiny.

This principle overturned the habits of ancient Babylon, of the Roman empires, and their like, under which populations were divided between a ruling oligarchical minority and its armed and other lackeys on the one side, and, on the other side, a mass of persons degraded in practice to the status of virtual human cattle. The notorious Physiocratic dogma of Dr. François Quesnay, is typical of modern attempts to continue the degradation of the great mass of the population to the status of human cattle. Although Quesnay was a shamelessly open defender of the feudal tradition, his argument did not differ in any essential either from that of England's John Locke and Bernard Mandeville, or of the Adam Smith whose famous *Wealth of Nations* was largely a plagiarism of the work of Physiocrats such as Quesnay.

Despite the use of religious warfare and other means, in the efforts by forces of the feudal tradition, to halt and reverse the development of the sovereign nation-state, the benefits of the introduction of the nation-state had been irreversible, even during two devastating world wars of the Twentieth Century, until that presently ongoing downturn, which was set into motion during the recent thirty-odd years. The new emphasis upon the development of infrastructure, the fostering of scientific and technological progress, the gradual freeing of the serfs, and related intentions of the nation-state institution, had resulted in a rise in life-expectancies, improvements in general demographic characteristics of households and of populations in general, and secular increase in the per-capita and per-square-kilometer productive powers of labor. The intentions expressed by the sovereign nation-state, by which one generation defines the future for one to two generations to come, spilled over into all forms of modern European society, and beyond.

However, because of the continuing legacy of the feudal tradition in modern Europe, the idea of the sovereign nation-state republic, created in Europe, was exported to find its first more fulsome expression in the creation and development of the U.S. republic in North America. It is in the development of the North American republic, from its colonial beginnings through the victory of President Abraham Lincoln, and into the last quarter of the Nineteenth Century, that the characteristic economic and related forms of intentions of the U.S. form of industrialized sovereign nation-state, were reflected, more and more in the development of Europe itself. The accelerated industrial development of Germany, Russia, and Japan, during the last quarter of the Nineteenth Century, and beyond, typify the impact of the 1861-1876 successes of the U.S. economy on the thinking and practice of nations in many parts of Eurasia.

Thus, although the development of the U.S. republic was set back severely by the French developments of 1789-1815, by the hostile actions of both the British monarchy and the Holy Alliance, President Lincoln's triumph over Lord Palmerston's Confederacy puppet sealed the character of the U.S. economy, until the downturn which was unleashed about three decades ago. During the Twentieth Century, following the 1901 assassination of President William McKinley, the American Tory faction seized control of the U.S. government and much of the economy besides. Franklin Roosevelt temporarily reversed that trend of 1901-1932, turning the U.S. back to the economic policies of the Lincoln legacy.

In all of these turns, despite the repeated reversals of many of the characteristic economic intentions of the U.S., the underlying character of those intentions survived, until the increasingly intensified efforts to uproot them, over the post-1965 period to date. It is through the understanding of the role of such *intentions*, rather than any statistical model, that the ebbs and flows of the U.S. economy are to be understood.

The crucial issue of *intention*, is the conflict between the heritage of Leibniz's notion of the general welfare principle, "life, liberty, and the pursuit of happiness," and the opposing, oligarchical notion of the ideas of the Confederacy, the ideas of the pro-slavery John Locke, "life, liberty, and property." The latter is typified today by the neo-Confederacy dogma of "shareholder value," currently enforced by the radically positivist, pro-racist majority of the U.S. Supreme Court.

The U.S. republic has been, from its beginning, a political battleground where the patriotic faction, committed to the principle of the general welfare, battles out the issues of economic, social, and foreign policy, with the opposing faction which Franklin Roosevelt identified as the American Tories. Since the 1966 election campaign of President Richard Nixon, it is the American Tories who have been increasingly in the saddles of U.S. political and economic power. The issue of the general welfare, to which the present administration, and the current majority of the U.S. Supreme Court are opposed, is the essential line of division between two opposing sets of axioms of U.S. foreign and domestic economic and social policy-making.

Just as the crisis of 1929-1933 brought President Franklin Roosevelt's advocacy of the general welfare to power, so the onrushing collapse of the U.S. economic policies of the past thirty-odd years, may signal another turn, back to the general welfare, like that of 1932-33. If that turn were to occur, the tendency would be for the U.S. to mobilize itself for the kind of cooperation with Eurasia which I have indicated.

That is a big "if," but it is the best option available to the world today.

Modern Economy

The principle of the general welfare, means that it must be the constitutional quality of *intention* of government, that it can make no law, or kindred convention, which might treat the majority of its population as virtually human cattle. The government's primary goals are to defend the integrity of the nation, in the interest of all of its people and their posterity, and to develop its territory in ways which promote the improvement of the demographic characteristics of the population as a whole, and also the average physical productive powers of labor.

These obligations of government define our planet as what the celebrated Vladimir Vernadsky defined as a noösphere. In other words, human creativity is deployed with the *intention* to maintain, transform, and improve the biosphere for human existence, and to accomplish this by means which include the *intention* for developing the general area through appropriate, large-scale and related infrastructural improvements, such as in water-management, power production, transportation, and so on.

The realization of the objectives of a noösphere, also requires the *intention* of an increase in the knowledge and productive powers of the population, largely through aid of scientific and technological progress. Only in such ways, through such *intentions*, could the general welfare be served.

This obliges government to place the primary emphasis of its *intentions* on the physical side of production as such, and to relegate the financial side of economic policy-shaping to those measures needed to facilitate trade and employment in fostering physically significant benefits. A sound economic system is, therefore, primarily a physical system, *by intention*, and a financial system only by derivation.

The required *intention* is the acceptance of the physical obligation to promote the general welfare through economic growth, obliges government to expend great efforts on behalf of its *intention* to promote the improvement of what we call basic economic infrastructure.

In practice, we find that such public works may be undertaken either solely by the efforts of government itself, or undertaken by privately owned public utilities acting according to regulations provided and maintained by government. For example, in effecting the recovery of the U.S. economy, about 40% of the growth stimulated by government action was in the area of basic economic infrastructure, and much of the remaining private sector's growth depended upon government-sponsored efforts such as the famous Tennessee Valley development. The choice of public or private ownership is of little significance, if either fulfills the intention more or less equally well. Franklin Roosevelt used both, as the example of the work of the Reconstruction Finance Corporation, illustrates that point. The matter of *intention of law* in these matters, lies in the mechanisms of regulation by which either private or public ownership of public works shall conduct their business.

In order to stimulate both public and private improvements, in must be the *intention* of society that prices must be set at levels which provide for maintenance of basic economic infrastructure and also capital improvements and high skill levels in production of goods and essential services. In other words, the general welfare requirement can not be served without *protectionist measures* of a type which can be ensured only through the authority of a sovereign nation-state's government.

The alternative to such *intentions*, is economic anarchy, and ruin. The globalizers' insistence that government not only abandon such *intentions*, but relinquish forever the authority to adopt such intentions, is the principal cause for the catastrophe in which the world is being plunged today.

For example, to rebuild the tattered and shattered world economy of today, large masses of credit must be created, and issued at low borrowing costs over periods of maturity ranging up to a quarter-century or more. With such public credit policies, and with protectionist measures of the sort which were widely employed during the 1945-1965 interval, large-scale improvements within increasing rates of productivity and technological progress, were available, even in regions as devastated as war-torn Europe.

Physical Economy and Eurasia

The catastrophic economic and related effects of globalization, have recently increased the recognition that only through new forms of closer cooperation among the leading nations of continental Eurasia, is there any visible opportunity for the general economic prosperity of continental Eurasia as a whole. A pattern of negotiations to this effect has been developing between nations of western continental Europe and Russia, together with increasing emphasis on wider cooperation with the great population centers of Central, East, Southeast and South Asia. In these matters, the need to provide security among all of the nations of Eurasia and the need for new forms and degrees of economic cooperation are inseparable practical concerns.

This emphasis upon Eurasia is not to the disadvantage of Africa, Australia, New Zealand, and the Americas. Quite the contrary, without a general economic recovery in continental Eurasia, there is no hope for the planet as a whole.

The national economies of Eurasia represent nations and cultures with significant differences in their characteristics. However, all share in common the need for similar benefits as measured in physical-economic terms. The most urgent elements of economic cooperation needed among this assortment as a whole, are preponderant emphasis on development of basic economic infrastructure, without which other improvements in the life of their populations were not possible, and large-scale and growing transfers of advanced productive technology from those places where fountains of such technology may be supplied, into areas in which the deficit of such technological infusions must be corrected.

The objectives of such cooperation are, generally, in the order of the required work of two generations, the coming quarter-century most urgently. This requires a system of long-term, relatively fixed parities among currencies, and upper limits on borrowing-costs and conditions, in which rates of between 1% and 2%, and simple interest, not compound, must prevail. The great bulk of the flows of physical capital will be concentrated in long-term credits, in the order of about twenty-five years. A quarter to one-half of the long-term credit and trade agreements will come under such provisions.

The experience under the original Bretton Woods agreements, during the period until about 1965, provides appropriate precedents. Study of the internal development of the U.S. economy during the difficult 1933-1945 interval, also provides relevant examples.

On the side of monetary and financial practices, this will require the forms of regulation which prevailed during the 1945-1965 interval, with initial emphasis on the more strict regulations of the 1945-1958 interval.

Additionally, special attention must be given to the lessons of the leading military and other great science-driver programs of the 1940-1965 interval, including the Kennedy manned Moon-landing program. The success of the recovery program required for Eurasia (and elsewhere) today, will depend upon the rapidity which can be achieved in science-driver modes of technological progress. When we consider the area of Eurasia as a whole, and also take into account the needs for technological progress among the dense population-areas of East, Southeast, and South Asia, the goals of recovery could not be achieved without aid of a greatly accelerated rate of technological progress. Only a science-driver strategy could ensure the acceleration of the rate of technological progress to needed levels.

This will require a twofold direction of change in the structural composition and education of the labor-force of Europe and the United States in particular. To fulfill our part in the partnership with the technologically less developed portions of the world, we must increase greatly the ration of the total labor-force employed in producing science and technology, and, shift the quality of employment of the remainder of the labor-force upward technologically. By these shifts in priorities for education, investment, and employment, we will be able to generate accelerated rates of increase of per-capita physical productive powers of labor in what is presently termed the advanced sector, and, thus, to generate higher rates of physical productivity into employment in the less advanced sectors of the world.

This means, physical-economic targets for the immediate quarter-century ahead, and monetary and financial policies designed to match the standards defined in physical-economic terms. To this end, we must clarify our intentions. If we do, we might imagine that President Franklin Roosevelt would be pleased with our intentions.

FIDELIO

Journal of Poetry, Science, and Statecraft

From the first issue, dated Winter 1992, featuring Lyndon LaRouche on "The Science of Music: The Solution to Plato's Paradox of 'The One and the Many,'" to the final issue of Spring/Summer 2006, a "Symposium on Edgar Allan Poe and the Spirit of the American Revolution," *Fidelio* magazine gave voice to the Schiller Institute's intention to create a new Golden Renaissance.

The title of the magazine, is taken from Beethoven's great opera, which celebrates the struggle for political freedom over tyranny. *Fidelio* was founded at the time that LaRouche and several of his close associates were unjustly imprisoned, as was the opera's Florestan, whose character was based on the American Revolutionary hero, the French General, Marquis de Lafayette.

Each issue of *Fidelio*, throughout its 14-year lifespan, remained faithful to its initial commitment, and offered original writings by LaRouche and his associates, on matters of, what the poet Percy Byssche Shelley identified as, "profound and impassioned conceptions respecting man and nature."

Back issues are now available for purchase through the Schiller Institute website:
http://schillerinstitute.org/about/order_form.html